A FLOATING
CITY OF PEASANTS

Migrant workers:
① Wang Yingmin
② Yang Aiguo
③ Yang Qun
④ Li Yanhong, Bai Chuiying,
  Wang Sujun, Li Gen, Ni Jianjun
⑤ Yang Chunming, Liu Dezhe
⑥ Yang Quan
⑦ Wang Hong
⑧ Cai Lulu, Yi Congcong
⑨ Li Suzhen
⑩ Li Guihong, Li Huaihong

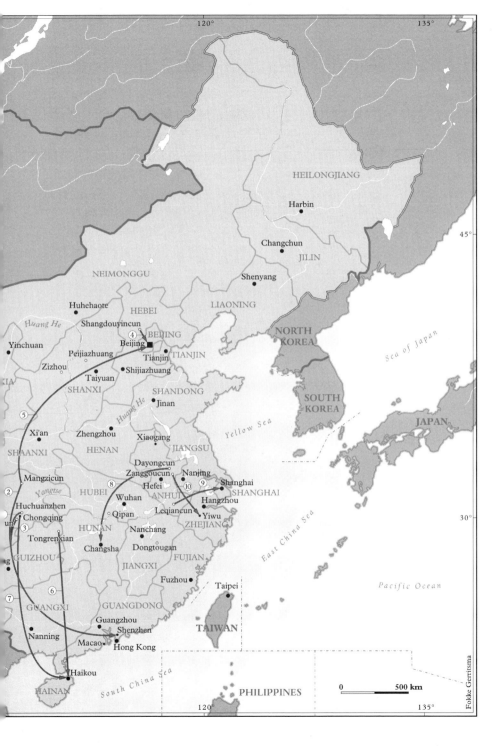

A FLOATING CITY OF PEASANTS

The Great Migration in Contemporary China

Floris-Jan van Luyn

Translated from the Dutch
by Jeannette K. Ringold

THE NEW PRESS

NEW YORK
LONDON

For information on the photographs in this book, see pages 211 to 214.

The translation and publication of this work have been made possible with financial support from the Foundation for the Production and Translation of Dutch Literature.

Originally published as *Een stad van boeren* in the Netherlands by Uitgeverij Prometheus / NRC Handelsblad
Published in the United States by The New Press, New York, 2008
Distributed by W. W. Norton & Company, Inc., New York

LIBRARY OF CONGRESS CATALOGING-IN-PUBLICATION DATA
Luyn, Floris-Jan van.
[Stad van boeren. English]
A floating city of peasants : the great migration in contemporary China / Floris-Jan van Luyn ; translated from the Dutch by Jeannette K. Ringold.
p.   cm.
ISBN 978-1-59558-138-9 (hc.)
1. Rural-urban migration—China.   2. Rural poor—China.   I. Title.
HB2114.A3L8913 2008
307.2'40951—dc22

2007035000

The New Press was established in 1990 as a not-for-profit alternative to the large, commercial publishing houses currently dominating the book publishing industry. The New Press operates in the public interest rather than for private gain, and is committed to publishing, in innovative ways, works of educational, cultural, and community value that are often deemed insufficiently profitable.

www.thenewpress.com
Composition by dix!

Printed in the United States of America

2   4   6   8   10   9   7   5   3   1

For Jan van Luyn
(1932–1997)

Contents

Introduction

By the Millions

The first time that I became fully aware of the limited rights of Chinese farmers was in the fall of 1991. I had just started my study of Chinese at a language institute in Beijing and had become friends with a young Chinese man whom Michael Cherney, one of this books's photographers, and I had met at a bus stop.

It wasn't the most obvious place to make friends, but while waiting for city bus 375, we started talking, we hit it off, and before we knew it we had suggested that he share lodgings with us so that we could learn from one another: he English and we Chinese. The young man, Cai Haitao, was enthusiastic.

The benefit was mutual, and the friendship that followed was genuine, as far as I could judge at the time. I still remember the naive excitement we felt when we finally found an apartment. What we did—students on grants living off-campus with a Chinese—was not allowed at the time. And that very disobedience made our adventure a success from the start.

Haitao turned out to be a nice young man—we enjoyed ourselves and learned a lot—but our being together did cause many problems. After collecting our rent, the landlady, who also had a concealed brothel in her home, became worried about the attention that we foreigners attracted. Curious neighbors kept asking questions; the police were informed and found our being together suspicious. When, after three months of increasing tensions, my money was stolen from a tin box hidden under the telephone table, our landlady was fed up. She suspected our Chinese roommate; we suspected her. We were asked to leave and were thrown out on the street.

This is how, in the heart of winter, we ended up in the stuffy and musty extra room of Haitao's parents' dilapidated courtyard house. There was no water, no toilet, and no heater, but we accepted the offer eagerly and thought it was terrific. The simpler the better, as far as we were concerned, and we felt that we had obtained front-row seats to watch the performance of "Real Life in a Chinese City."

And it certainly was real. Very soon we got an uncensored picture of the Cais' lives, and that was sobering. The family had a peasant girl as a servant in their home, and from her we learned that our friendly host family had a less cordial side as well.

The girl, whose name was Xiaolu, acted as the house slave. She did everything: cleaning, cooking, making beds, getting water, keeping the fires of the coal-burning stoves going; she spent all day working for the Cais.

In return she received not money but annoyed reactions. The Cais felt that Xiaolu did not do her work well. They felt that she was slow and lazy. Moreover, Haitao's father argued, "we've given her an opportunity. Without us she'd still be standing in the mud up to her ankles; without us she'd still be a peasant girl without a future." She should above all be grateful.

I didn't understand it at all. Xiaolu, the peasant's daughter from Shaanxi, likely had another point of view; you could tell that from her face, but no one asked her opinion. During the rare moments of rest in her exceedingly busy existence, she dared to tell me, in a whisper, that she longed to go home. Coming to the city, she confessed almost inaudibly, was the greatest mistake she'd ever made. The Cais were distant relatives of her father (that is why the Cais didn't feel obliged to pay her), and that had seemed in their favor. Perhaps they could even provide her with a step up to a better life. But she couldn't have made a worse choice.

Xiaolu's story certainly stimulated my curiosity. I wanted to know where people like her came from and what that "hard existence" on the land and the migration to the city really meant. Of course, Xiaolu wasn't the only migrant worker. Millions had gone before her, and many millions would follow her. What made Chinese peasants like Xiaolu decide to leave life in their native region and trade it for an uncertain existence in the big city?

During the trips that I have since made through China, my fascination with the peasants has increased. First it was the raw excitement of the tangible exoticism of the countryside; later I felt a bizarre historical awareness. It was bizarre because, confronted with the peasants, I thought I had found something that had all but disappeared in the city: remnants of Communist China as it must have been before the advance of capitalism—including shared ideals and signs of patriotism and mutual brotherhood, but also over-the-top megalomania, mass hysteria, and the never-ending misery that I'd read so much about. The peasants' lives were a lesson in recent history.

But there was and still is a lesson for the future. The masses to whom Mao Zedong and his political successors owe their legitimacy still vegetate on the land; they now number 850 million. The more you concentrate on that immense agricultural hinterland and its population, the clearer it becomes that the peasants, despite their poverty and deprivation, or perhaps just because of it, have a significant role in determining the future of China.

The deeply rooted desire to escape that poverty impels more and more peasants to leave the land. They find employment in the city, where there is a huge demand for cheap labor. And thanks to the constant availability of this floating population of migrant peasants, China's economy can take giant steps forward. In other words, China's skyscrapers are becoming taller, its highways wider, its airports greater in number, its computers more modern;

and its market increases constantly. But the strength of this renewal derives from the peasants who, on the land, in the factories, in construction, or, like Xiaolu, as servants, respond to China's need for modernization. Without the peasants, there would be no modernization.

Is this a remarkable development? Perhaps not. Europe has its guest workers from Turkey and Morocco; the United States has its workers from Mexico. Almost every country has guest workers. But the size of the migration in China is exceptional. Nowhere in the world and never before in history has a country had to deal with as great a demographic shift as that taking place in China. The rate at which the Chinese peasants are leaving their land—20 million annually, according to the latest Chinese census—is so high that not only are the cities becoming overcrowded, but the farmland is more and more often left fallow.

"Money no longer comes from the soil," say the farmers. That was not always the case. For a brief period at the end of the 1970s, when the communes were disbanded, those working the land seemed to fare better. Farmers were once again allowed to earn money and sell their products on the free market. But that progress fell off again after a little more than a decade. Decentralization, pursuit of profit, and a lack of good, enforceable rules caused a new crisis among the peasants in the mid-1990s. By and large, taxes and levies were unreasonably high, which caused more and more peasants to gradually spend their recently saved money. Many of them became disillusioned.

This is why the peasants found their way to the city. Chinese specialists estimate their number between 120 million and 150 million, but the numbers are probably higher. They still arrive by the thousands at the train stations in the big cities to find their way as construction workers, factory workers, cooks, waiters and waitresses, hairdressers, au pairs, or prostitutes in the countless construction sites, factories, restaurants, beauty parlors, city families, and brothels. This book is about these people.

Together the floating population of migrant workers is the flip side of the shiny façade that China so often presents. Progress has its price, and it is paid primarily by the peasants, knowingly and without much complaint because in the end even they profit.

"The peasants' opinion does not matter," party bureaucrats said for years on end, because "peasants are uneducated." It is a truth that is still considered reasonable by many a party member because the party has convinced itself that "we have the best interests of the people at heart and we know what is good for them." In short, the peasants don't even need to be heard. Everything will turn out all right under the superb leadership of the party. Just as during the centuries that preceded communism, the result is that most peasants keep quiet.

But it is a silent mass harboring repressed hostility. The peasants do have an opinion, though they keep it to themselves. This is how it has always been.

The pioneer peasants who reach the city have been kicked around all their lives, but in their new surroundings they are learning to stand up for themselves. They are becoming more articulate and realize increasingly that their achievements are thanks mainly to themselves and not to the party. And many of them return to their native regions with that infectious confidence. In this way they feed the hinterland, both economically and psychologically.

"I collect their garbage, but I get treated like a dog," says one of those self-aware peasants profiled in this book. He has had fourteen years of school and believes that he is smarter than many of the people whose garbage he collects. He is especially sensitive to the city dwellers' condescension. "I may look like a country bumpkin, but I'm not stupid," he says angrily.

Many migrant workers whose voices are heard in this book are angry. But surprisingly, no one gives up. For each of these peasants, the desire for economic prosperity, no matter how difficult to reach, outweighs all humiliation. The Chinese have a special capacity to persevere and to survive; migrant workers don't give up easily. This talent to keep going on against one's better judgment is as remarkable as it is admirable.

• • •

None of the opinions and experiences of the people whose voices are heard in this book are exceptional. They are not stories of heroes or individuals who have served their country in distinct ways according to either Chinese or foreign standards. They are simple souls, innocent beings, sometimes children, just following larger trends made possible by politics or started by like-minded people.

In this book their stories and portraits alternate with observations—about the desire or need to leave the villages, about the need to become integrated in the cities, and about the difficulties of doing so.

All these stories were recorded in the latter part of the 1990s and the first years of the new century. Even though the reality of these people may have changed since I visited them, new migrant workers keep coming. For the time being, this story has not ended.

The countryside is emptying and the cities are becoming overcrowded. The peasants move from one job to the next. Their combined hard work is productive. Together all these migrant laborers represent a powerful group of innovators; together they are building the symbols of progress. They form a floating city of peasants.

Beijing/The Hague, May 2006

A FLOATING
CITY OF PEASANTS

对

Prologue

Wishful Thinking

The Chinese word for "migrant workers," *liudong renkou*, carries the image of rapids. *Liu* means "stream" or "flood"; *liudong* means "in motion" or "to stream"; and *renkou* means "population." Loosely translated: the streaming or floating population.

Liudong renkou does not have a neutral meaning. It is definitely not a babbling or peacefully meandering brook. The peasants don't come trickling into the cities in small groups or one by one. Instead, this stream of migrants that consists of uprooted peasants is seen by many Chinese as huge and relentless, a tidal wave.

This is not a friendly description, but almost nowhere in China are the migrant workers received with open arms. According to those who feel beleaguered, the peasants are first and foremost a burden. Trains are full to overflowing; buses are packed, cities are becoming filthier; slums spring up overnight. In short, the cities are becoming overcrowded. And yet the cities cannot function without the peasants. The peasants—who learned to sow and harvest from childhood on—build, feed, and serve the cities. Governing them is perhaps the only thing they don't do. As far as Chinese bureaucrats are con-

cerned, that should definitely remain the way it is. They see the migrant workers as a necessary evil—necessary to the economy but harmful to the legal
order.

Those representing advocates and opponents of the migrant influx fight to
be heard by the highest authorities. Policy makers at one extreme of the spec-
trum want total abolishment of all regulations that restrict peasants coming to
the cities. Others want total prohibition and extreme restrictions to exclude
peasants from the cities. The majority opinion is that the peasants should be
allowed to come, as long as the situation remains manageable.

But how do you manage a deluge?

The numbers are dizzying. No one can say exactly how many Chinese have
exchanged their land for one of China's 670 cities. According to Chinese estimates, the numbers may be between 120 million and 150 million. But how
accurate can an estimate be when it has a margin of error the size of the population of California?

Chinese statistics are as soft as butter. They are only as reliable as the people
who draw them up. The numbers seldom reflect the facts but are often a personal assessment of interests. Independent testing does not exist. Many local
party bureaucrats feel under great pressure to comply with the party's quotas
for population policy. If the National Bureau of Statistics reports that between
May and October of 2001, 62,000 errors were discovered in data delivered by
the provinces, that is significant. Everyone knows that China is not eager to tell
the truth.

In the most populous country under the sun, it is easy to overlook a million
people or so. But who in China will admit that? The latest Chinese census, that
of 2000, was "99 percent accurate," claims Gu Chongzhou, deputy director of
the National Bureau of Statistics in Beijing and a man who helped to manage
the greatest survey ever seen by humankind.

It was the fifth time that the People's Republic had organized a census, and considering its magnitude, it certainly was an enormously difficult job. The result of the census showed that 1,295,330,000 Chinese were living in the country at that moment. In the preceding twenty years (the last population census was carried out in 1982), an average of 21 million Chinese were born and 8 million died annually. The population growth for that period was equal to adding one Illinois per year: 12.8 million Chinese per year.

It is barely possible to comprehend these numbers. But what it actually means is that while you take a deep breath, one more Chinese child is born. Every 1.5 seconds means another child: fifty-seven thousand people a day. During the ten days of the census, while more than 6 million census takers were out doing their work, another half million Chinese children were born!

Despite the massiveness of the undertaking, Gu feels that the answers collected during those days are reliable. "Misuse of information is not permitted. Punishing someone afterward for something admitted to the census takers [about violations of population policies] was forbidden," he says.

Gu seems a trusting man. But the existence of a prohibition does not guarantee good behavior, certainly not in China. In a society that does not shrink from using totalitarian measures to enforce controversial population and residence policies, few people must have felt compelled to risk punishment or a fine for reporting a child too many or an unauthorized residence. That is why in China, collecting even simple information and getting answers to simple questions such as "How many children do you have?" or "Where do you live?" are overwhelmingly difficult.

A warning from Wang Zhongyu, who was responsible for the national census, says enough as far as that is concerned. During a preparatory meeting of the heads of the provincial bureaus who would manage the census, Wang Zhongyu called on them to do the obvious. Civil servants were ordered to obey the rules. "The census may not fail," said Wang. "We must collect the correct information," an imperative that was not self-evident. "Indirect fines after census interviews are not permitted. . . . The answers are confidential and may not be used to punish people for mistakes they have made in the past."

But even after the census, there still is great uncertainty about the large group of unregistered children (estimated at 200 million) who should not have been born, according to the one-child policy, and about the millions of peasants who migrated to the cities in contravention of the rules of Chinese residency policy.

The problem, as many peasants explain when asked, is not the central government but arrogant and often corrupt local civil servants. These party bureaucrats have long since forfeited the trust of the people, to the extent that it was present at all. But of all people, these hated civil servants were the ones who went door-to-door to collect "honest answers" about the state of the population.

Why is it so important to know how many Chinese there are? After all, would a few million more or less make a difference in the overpopulation problem? The party bureaucrats want to know, and that is a good thing.

The number of Chinese who live on the land, leave the land, and migrate to the city has great consequences not only for China but also for the rest of the world. Western champions of democracy and openness need consider for only a moment the consequences of unrestricted freedom of movement for all Chinese to realize how troublesome that freedom would be. If we assume that 10 percent of the Chinese make use of this right and seek a home outside China (in view of the present state of China's economy, this is not an unreasonable percentage), where will these 130 million people end up? The problems faced by the Chinese party bureaucrats are of this nature and magnitude.

The peasants are needed for the economic development of the country— they build the future—but the mass that all of them form is large and unmanageable. The situation of the peasants is unstable, and the central government long ago lost its grasp on the development of their well-being.

The fear of completely abolishing peasant immobility thus originates from the party's survival instinct. If it does nothing, then it endorses its own downfall; most party bureaucrats have by now realized that if the peasant mass is rubbed the wrong way for a long enough time, it will revolt sooner or later. It wasn't for nothing that Wen Jiabao, during his first speech as prime minister in March 2003, called the improvement of the peasants' position "the central task and the most important goal" of the Chinese government. And since that time Prime Minister Wen has treated several migrants to unexpected inspection visits to find out how they are really doing.

Knowing the extent of the problem is half the work, according to the Chinese think tanks. Where do the peasants come from, what do they want, what do they do, what can they do, and do they really constitute a danger? Foreign institutes have joined the discussion, but they, too, are unable to gather accurate data. Their estimates of the peasant invasion are often less restrained, and the picture they paint is an even greater cause for worry (this explains the Chinese reticence to reveal accurate data).

At the end of 2002, the United Nations calculated that another 200 million peasants will leave their farmland for the city between 2000 and 2010. The Asian Development Bank assumes that during the same period there will be 300 million more peasants in the cities (more than the population of the United States).

The mass migration taking place in China is already the largest in the history of humanity.

Beijing has allocated significant financial resources for extensive studies to find out what the consequences of this migration really are. There is much discussion and worry about the subject. Whole think tanks are involved in the problem, and with increasing frequency there are countrywide meetings of scholars and policy makers who study the question. The wildest projections have been made, and all the statistics are going through the roof.

Everyone in Beijing is letting the numbers get to them. For years economists kept harping on the importance of economic growth. At the end of the

1990s, *baoba*—"protect the eight"—was an important economic concept. Eight percent economic growth had become a very serious matter. Less growth was irresponsible. According to somber predictions, with economic growth below "the eight," the country would be irrevocably damned. The lower the prognosis for growth, the more disastrous the image of the future.

Foreign economists eagerly went along with that doom scenario. They did place the critical boundary somewhat lower, at 4 percent growth, but the peasants would then migrate to the cities in even greater numbers. Under "the four" would mean revolution in China.

Fortunately there were still individuals who kept a cool head, for example, Li Yiyuan. "That 'eight' contained a large quantity of *shuifen* [mist]," he says. Li is a professor of quantitative economics at Qinghua University in Beijing, and he knows his figures. "For party bureaucrats, realizing target figures is not a question of being able to but of wanting to," he says. "If the Chinese government desires eight percent economic growth, it happens. In this country, target figures are realized because they are set by the government, regardless of the cost. And that's final." The Chinese forecasts consist of a good portion of fantasy and wishful thinking. In 2005, China's economic growth was supposed to be 9.3 percent.

However, this does not prevent some Chinese demographers from being pessimistic. They have very different worries about the population migration and point out, for instance, the unbalanced composition of the Chinese population and its consequences. More than half of the migrants are young men under the age of twenty-five. These demographers wonder what will happen when large groups of young men leave the rural areas. First of all, in the hinterland this will create a society that consists solely of women and the elderly to work the land and take care of the children who were left behind. It is not until they are in the city that many young men discover that by leaving home they have diminished their chances of finding a female life partner.

Most male peasants are used to that situation because there is a shortage of women in China anyway. A combination of tradition (abortion or murder of the baby after determining that it is female), poverty (a need for sons), pride (continuation of the paternal family line), and the one-child policy have led to a surplus of boys in China.

According to the 2000 census, 107 boys were born for every 100 girls that year, slightly above the international average. But in some areas, especially in the hinterland, that ratio is 117 to 100. This explains the millions of unregistered peasants' daughters who did come into the world but are not registered anywhere.

According to some radical demographers, this also means that so many unmarried peasants populate the outskirts of the big cities that a revolt cannot be ruled out because the peasants are after not money but women. Referring to history, they point out the size of that threat. In 1851, similar population ratios led to an armed attack on the established order, an offensive known as the Nian Rebellion.

Zhang Yi, a demographer at the Chinese Academy for Social Sciences, believes that the disaster scenario from that time could also happen today. He reminds us that there were dissatisfied "male communities" of unmarried peasants at that time. From sheer boredom they formed gangs, totaling about fifty thousand men, and were able to take control of a region the size of France. It took the Qing rulers as many as seventeen years to crush that rebellion completely. It is an unlikely hypothesis for the future, but it illustrates how fearful the leaders and their advisers are about the peasant invasion that, according to some, has already started.

Fortunately for the peasants, it looks like these doomsayers may be wrong. More and more progressive Chinese thinkers see the positive side of the peasants' metamorphosis. One of these scholars is Ruan Daching, a Beijing sociologist. He believes that the giant step that China is undergoing with the mass migration will only benefit the nation. "Just imagine," he says excitedly. "It's the liberation of the decade. For centuries the Chinese were sentenced to their land. Being born in a peasant village always meant that you would die there, too. No one ever thought of changing that system. It was so terribly unfair. But just see what is happening now, now that the peasants are free to come and go as they please—it means that they can finally dream about the future and that their dreams can come true."

A Floating City of Peasants

City Builders

(Shenzhen, Fuyong)

No city in China exerts as great an attraction on migrant workers as Shenzhen. This city of millions on the border with Hong Kong has in less than twenty years grown from a sleepy fishing village to China's most successful special economic zone—the name the Chinese government has given to the five cities and provinces that filled a pioneering role in the early days of the development of China's market economy.

In those areas there was a constant need for cheap and unskilled labor. For years migrant workers were able to get jobs right away, and it is said that the chance of succeeding in Shenzhen is greater than anywhere else in China. After all, Shenzhen was built by migrant workers, and they are the mainstay of the city's flourishing economy.

The largest factories in Shenzhen are the workplaces of most peasant women. Nowhere else do so many peasant women work as in those factories where demand for precision labor is greatest. According to the factory bosses, women work more carefully than men. They can spool thread, solder resistors, position picture tubes, assemble toy trains, decorate Christmas tree ornaments, and build miniature ships.

Sometimes Yang Qun feels rather artistic. The plastic animals that she paints are for export. She thinks that's wonderful—her work, in the homes of strangers in foreign countries.

Emancipating thoughts are not at the basis of this image; the reasoning is that women are simply more sensitive and work with greater concentration—their hands are soft and careful. In those factories men are considered coarse and not careful, their hands rough and not sensitive. They are better at sawing, hauling, chopping, and dumping. There is no lack of role-stereotype reinforcement here.

Whoever enters these bastions of women's work doesn't only see tired employees who have to perform the same task for too long at wages that are too low, but also sees many women with a striking feeling of self-respect. Although they are seldom in charge, on the shop floor of these city factories many women develop an awareness of independence that most peasant women do not get at home.

Yang Qun is one of these women. She is twenty-three years old, has already been in Shenzhen for six years, and therefore is the oldest and most experienced woman in her department. The factory where she has worked from the start makes models of animals. "When you do the same thing over and over for a long time, then you sometimes can't stand it anymore." But the models that she paints are always different. "You paint two hundred ducks, and then five hundred dogs." It doesn't drive Yang crazy; on the contrary, "if I could choose, I would do the same work again." It sounds too good to be true. But it isn't, she says. "I even feel a little bit artistic. And it's more varied than in an electronics factory. There women turn out the same games, day in, day out." She knows this because her own workplace is adjacent to an electronics factory. She speaks almost daily with the young women who work there.

Yang Qun does not feel that her years in Shenzhen have been unpleasant at all. She left the countryside behind wholeheartedly and doesn't long to go back home. "I've never been afraid," she says. "I've always been sure that I wanted to get away from the land. I felt confined there." She finds it remarkable that her parents supported her in her decision. "They know that I'm independent and can take care of myself." They have never expressed any concern about her independence. "I enjoy my freedom."

Yang Qun earns 800 yuan ($100) per month. She keeps most of the money for herself, unless her family in Sichuan asks for help. "In the beginning, my parents were short of money. One of my brothers went to senior high school and there was a great lack of money. That's why I sent them my salary." That problem no longer exists, since her brothers work in the city, too.

She herself was not able to finish high school because of a shortage of money, but Yang Qun says that this disappointment is more than outweighed by the freedom that she has gained in her life away from the countryside. She is also sure that she wants to remain in Shenzhen for the time being. All of her classmates from junior high school who stayed in the village are already married. "And most of them have children," she says, horrified. She can't bear to think about it. "At the present I don't want to have a husband," she says decidedly. "Men impose their opinions, and before you know it you've lost your freedom and you're at their beck and call." Perhaps, says Yang Qun, her school friends like a predictable and dependent life. "Well, I don't. I prefer not to be dependent on anyone."

Now that she earns her own money, she can do what she wants. Every month, almost half of her income goes for food and clothing. "I like clothes," she says. Above her bed in a barracks for factory workers a forest of blouses is drying on hangers. She is proud of them. "For the rest I'm frugal." She doesn't smoke or drink and doesn't go out. "Those flashing disco lights make me dizzy."

As the "oldest" on the floor, she has the best spot in the ramshackle apartment: the bottom bed in a four-person room, far away from the noisy stairwell. The newcomers sleep near the exit; those who have just arrived don't even have a room and sleep in the hallway.

One of the latest arrivals sits nervously on the edge of her bed. She radiates a newcomer's uncertainty. On her lap lies bright yellow knitting, and her eyes are constantly cast down. The red suitcase under her bed looks new, and apparently all her belongings are still inside it; her bed is still empty, as opposed to those of her roommates.

Anyone who wants to, says Yang Qun, gets to know new people in no time at all. The newcomers don't have to be lonely for long. All the girls have gone through the same thing and understand the problems of a beginning migrant worker: homesickness, the pressure of work, and exhaustion. "Only girls with guts come here," says Yang Qun. "If you don't have guts, then you stay home." Her new roommate will manage, she thinks.

One day, says Yang Qun, she will return to her parental home. "When people ask who I am, I say that I'm a peasant, even if I don't feel like one. But my ID says that I'm a peasant, and I'll always remain one." Yang Qun does not want to change her status for that of a city dweller—if she could ever afford to pay for it. "City dwellers have so many problems. They are unemployed; the government enterprises go bankrupt; they lose their guaranteed income and

Yang Qun's roommates are her friends. They go shopping, cook their meals, and eat together. For rest and privacy Yang Qun and her girlfriends use the curtains around their beds. If they are closed, everyone knows that it means don't disturb. And that is respected.

their right to housing. In the country no one is bothered by that. We can fall back on the land. The land is our safety net. But I must confess that I've never used a shovel to turn the soil." She laughs exuberantly.

SHREWD AND FRUGAL

Shenzhen is above all a city of falling and picking yourself up again. Ups and downs go hand in hand. Some peasants manage to find work right away or to start their own business; most take longer or never succeed.

"The beginning is the most difficult," says Wang Yingmin. "How do you as a poverty-stricken peasant gain the trust of your potential financial backers? That's what it's about. Once you have their trust, there are no more problems. And when you have money, everything goes smoothly. Then everyone believes in your capacity to earn, and they dare to invest in you." But how do you take the first step? "Most peasants aren't even capable of that."

Yingmin should know. He has a peasant background, but despite his age (he is twenty-eight), he left the countryside a long time ago. Yingmin, a short, stocky man with a round, chubby face, has by now become a successful entrepreneur who rides a shiny motorcycle, possesses not one but two cell phones, and almost always eats out. "By now I feel like a real Shenzhen resident," he says, truly proud. "I'm no longer a peasant in anyone's eyes. I've got more common sense than most people who are from here. Shenzhen is a place where you are valued for your achievements and for nothing else. That's why it's so unique. There is no place in China where the difference between the local population and the *waidiren*, the people from the countryside, is as unimportant as here. The people from elsewhere *are* Shenzhen.

"Of course there are rules that I have to comply with as an ex-peasant. For example, my child has to pay more tuition, and I'll have to purchase a residence permit of 20,000 yuan [$2,480] for him. I've got that money ready. I don't think that's unfair, for we do, after all, live in a special economic zone,

Yingmin doesn't show his wealth. "The migrants know that I'm one of them." But he can't leave his motorcycle. He uses it to drop by the projects where his men are working. Without getting off he urges them on, settles what needs to be done, and then tears off again at full throttle.

where different rules apply than elsewhere in the country. But I never considered living anywhere else because I am convinced that it's much more difficult for peasants in other cities. In most cities the rights of the local population are enormous; they claim the best jobs, regardless of their abilities. Not here. In Shenzhen everyone has the same opportunity."

Yingmin lights a cigarette. He inhales, self-satisfied. "I've never smoked expensive cigarettes," he says. He sounds slightly defiant, as if he is disclosing the secret of his success. But that may be true. Apparent modesty characterizes Yingmin, and except for his motorcycle and his cell phones, by which he loves to be interrupted frequently, he doesn't show his wealth. With his crew cut, white dress shirt, gray slacks and belt with a gold-colored Playboy logo on the buckle, pager on his hip, and imitation leather men's handbag pressed under his upper arm, he looks a dime a dozen. "There are many people who spend more than they can afford. They smoke a 30 yuan [$3.70] pack, are very generous, but cannot live up to the wealth that they display. That's disastrous." Yingmin says that success is a combination of "modesty and patience."

Yingmin didn't have to think for long about trading Huchuanzhen, his parental home in Sichuan, for an uncertain future in Shenzhen. "There was no doubt, staying in the country was the stupidest thing you could do. Practically no one in our village remained behind," he says. "We frittered away our time in Huchuanzhen. There was nothing to do there. I didn't care at all for school. I was short and thin and had a hard time. I wanted to get away. My sister said, 'You'll amount to nothing. You're lazy and you're wasting your life.' Well, she's had to take back those words. 'Someday you'll come and beg me for help,' I said, and that's what happened. Practically my whole family is in Shenzhen now, at my expense. My two older brothers, my older sister, and my father are all here. My mother died when I was seven. Only my youngest sister stayed behind; she watches over the parental house and our land." Neighbors work the land ("because agricultural land should not lie fallow") by order of Yingmin, who pays for it.

Yingmin made the journey from Huchuanzhen to Shenzhen together with an uncle. Yingmin was seventeen at the time. "I was really nervous," he remembers. Fortunately, his uncle was there to show him the way: "not a nice man, but a godsend."

During his first four months in Shenzhen, Yingmin earned a living by digging ditches. "Can you imagine? I was a little 106-pound guy digging ditches. All day long." He didn't really mind it. "It gave me time to reflect about the future." The deeper the ditches that he had to dig, the more convinced he became that he wanted to earn his money with his head and not with his hands. He never wanted to go back home.

Life in Shenzhen suited him. "I found life here much more pleasant than at home. We lived in a tent, ate a fat piece of pork once a week, and started at 14 yuan [$1.74] per month. In the third month, I was already earning 200 yuan and in four months, I had saved 1,000 yuan [$124]—more than I had ever dreamed."

Brimming with self-assurance, Yingmin returned to Huchuanzhen. In that short time, he had earned more money than any of his classmates, and he wanted to talk about that at home. Moreover, he had plans; he wanted to spend his just-earned money for a noble goal: He was going to finish school.

But at home a disappointment awaited him. Yingmin had again obediently taken his place at the school desk, but he was still a poor student. His five best friends managed to pass their examinations and were admitted to senior high school. Yingmin was kept back. "My friends were very happy, but I had the feeling that they looked down on me. I was so disappointed about my own performance, but especially because I think that an education doesn't prove that you're smarter than other people." It still bothers him. "I had much more experience of life than these boys."

Yingmin decided not to sulk for long, packed his bags, and went back to Shenzhen. He never went back to Huchuanzhen. "I've severed all ties with it."

When Yingmin returned to Shenzhen in the summer of 1991, he resolved never to leave it again. "I wanted to become rich." He had no papers; there were special rules for the Shenzhen economic zone, and therefore he remained there illegally. "During that time I was picked up several times for being illegal. Nowadays it's all much simpler. Now I have friends who can help me with everything. I know most of the police, and they wouldn't think of bothering me." Yingmin rubs his thumb and index finger together to indicate that it had cost him a considerable sum.

"In the beginning, I didn't feel welcome in Shenzhen. That was strange because we *waidiren*, people from the outside, were badly needed. The local population always sneered at us. They would jokingly call us *beilao*, 'northerners.' But to tell you the truth, the local population is much more stupid than we. They were simple fishermen, and today they are the ones who earn least. They can't do anything. They can't manage money. Without the peasants from the countryside, Shenzhen would never have become such a prosperous city."

The first months after his return to Shenzhen, Yingmin installed electric cables. "At that time there was practically no infrastructure. Work was available for the asking." In no time at all, Yingmin set up his own business. That was in 1994. "I earned 20,000 yuan [$2,480] per year with my trade in building materials." With that money, he and a fellow villager started a brokerage in train tickets. "I thought, so many migrants—they'll want to go home sometime." From experience, Yingmin knew that train tickets were hard to get: "long lines, bad tickets, and hard seats to Beijing." He bought the tickets in Guangzhou, the capital of south China's province of Guangdong, and sold them for a higher price in Shenzhen. "The business ran very smoothly," says Yingmin, until his partner took off with 10,000 yuan ($1,240). "That was two hundred train tickets; I lost all my money." Yingmin says that he never saw that friend again. "I'll get him sometime. To this day, that guy hasn't dared to return to Huchuanzhen because my friends will make mincemeat of him."

This setback was of short duration. "The good thing about Shenzhen is that you can sink really low and yet start again. No bankruptcy is permanent here." His money was gone, but meanwhile there were loyal business friends who were willing to lend some money to an enterprising man like Yingmin. And so he started a new business as a broker between peasants looking for work and contractors. "An opportunity. In no time at all, I was employing two hundred migrant workers." Yingmin had many contacts, his clients trusted him, and money started flowing in steadily.

But instead of marking time and living off his newly earned riches (within a year he was earning 68,000 yuan), Yingmin opened three restaurants—long, narrow places with fluorescent lighting, tables, and stools. Peasants have to eat, he thought. But none of the restaurants attracted customers, and within a few months he was bankrupt once again. "The very nature of restaurants is difficult—there is a lot of competition," he says.

Again Yingmin was flat broke, and again he borrowed money. "I did have to nag people because my rich friends were starting to doubt my entrepreneurial ability," he says without self-mockery. He still has the construction firm that he set up with that last round of investment. "I don't complain," says Yingmin, "but I'm taking it a bit easier. I now have a girlfriend and a child, and I take fewer risks."

Yingmin's apartment is on the third floor of an apartment building in a fenced housing complex for factory workers. It borders the electronics factory, and when the midday bell tolls, the sound of an amplified gong, a stream of young women in blue factory jackets spills outside through the adjacent factory gate.

They mingle with other young people—old people are practically absent from this district of Shenzhen—each group of which is wearing jackets of a different color. Every factory or division has its own color. They walk over the grounds in small groups, arm in arm, holding hands, or leaning on each other. Each and every one of the young women wears pants with flared legs and shoes with platform soles, as if these were part of their uniform.

Yingmin knows that they are on their lunch break, out to get a breath of fresh air and recover from the monotonous work on the factory floor. It isn't until the factory siren sounds the end of lunch break—it's barely half an hour—and the blue crowd has returned to its workplace, that silence returns to the housing complex.

"She's also from Sichuan. She worked in one of my restaurants, and that's how it happened," says Yingmin as he introduces me to his girlfriend, a woman in Mickey Mouse pajamas and curlers. She is busy taking care of her newborn baby and ignores the visitor. Yingmin says that they never bothered to get married, despite the fact that Chinese law does not tolerate unmarried couples. But Yingmin couldn't care less about such rules. Moreover, he feels that this says nothing about his fidelity to the mother of his son. "In Shenzhen you don't talk about love. You look at what you have with each other. I usually go to bed very late and spend a lot of time with my friends. My girlfriend goes to bed much earlier than I. We usually see each other only in passing."

Yingmin is not a family man, especially not when it concerns distant relatives. "Quite often relatives from Sichuan come and ask me for help." Yingmin knows that many migrant workers have the same experience. As soon as they seem to achieve success, a parade of family members and fellow villagers follows in hopes of a getting a recommendation or a share of the just-acquired prosperity. "In the beginning I offered them help. Every month a few people would come. Then they lived here until they could support themselves. But it's endless. These are people whom I know only indirectly. Now I just give them something to eat and 100 yuan. After that they have to figure things out themselves."

Yingmin feels that the newcomers among the migrant workers are often lazy. "They come without plans. They are uneducated. They fantasize all day long about the future, about a rich boss who selects them, but they do nothing. It was different in my time. Things don't happen by themselves. There is plenty of work, but you have to pay for success.

"In Shenzhen," says Yingmin, "everything revolves around money. Old traditions like hospitality or precious friendships no longer exist. If you don't pay, nothing happens. It can't be helped." Everyone is busy, and there is less and less time for social contacts that have no commercial importance. "Nowadays friendships have meaning only if they are to your advantage. I think it's a shame, but in the end I can't blame anyone; I'm busy myself."

FAT FROM DRINKING

The afternoon consists of work, or what passes for it. Yingmin takes food to his workers. A number of them are working on the renovation of a shopping complex on the outskirts of Fuyong. They get a pot of rice and vegetables that Yingmin's wife has put in the back of a pickup truck. In no time the hungry and sweaty men have gulped down their meals. There is loud burping, a bottle of beer is passed around from mouth to mouth, and then it's time to get back to work.

Next Yingmin hurries to inspect an addition to a small Taiwanese factory. It lies on recently developed land on the coast, just outside Shenzhen, and the pickup truck with its open back bumps and jolts to it in forty-five minutes. If you look carefully, you can see one of the container ports of Hong Kong sparkle across the water on the horizon.

The Taiwanese factory boss is waiting for Yingmin in a garden chair at the entrance of the complex together with his *ernai*, his second wife, and his children. "That's quite usual here," says Yingmin before his car turns onto the factory site. "Of course his Taiwanese wife knows nothing about this." The factory boss is in a bad mood and immediately starts calling Yingmin names. The construction of the building is not progressing fast enough for him. He gesticulates back and forth furiously, from Yingmin to an unfinished outside wall. Yingmin puts up with it, accepts the criticism stoically, and promises improvement. "The customer is king," he says later, professionally. In no way does he show that the Taiwanese boss's accusations have affected him. "As a contractor you're cursed out so often. If you got angry every time, you wouldn't be suitable for this work."

A little later Yingmin proudly shows a gray building down the road. It was built by him too and looks like a dilapidated storage building. But doll clothes are being made there. In a large hall filled with sewing machines, dozens of young women are working silently in the production line, pulling these mini-garments through the rattling machines. Sweat drips from their foreheads; the place is stifling hot.

Adjacent are the dormitories of the *nügong*, the female migrant workers. The rooms are plastered with concrete and include a squatting toilet. Eight bunk beds fit into each room, and each one is screened off by mosquito netting. Here and there a head or a foot sticks out; these are the young women who just finished their shift and may rest. They seem listless. The porches in the factory courtyard are filled with just-washed clothes hanging to dry. Because of the heat and the humidity of south China, the process takes a long time.

It is not a place that makes one feel cheerful. The factory is so remote that possible amusement in Fuyong or Shenzhen is out of reach for the workers. But their situation has no effect on Yingmin. "They work for a few years and then they go home with a filled wallet. That can be managed."

Yingmin himself doesn't exactly lead a tiring life. He usually stays up late, plays mah-jongg with his friends, has a foot massage in one of the popular pedicure salons, and sleeps very late. "Most people see only the outside. In their eyes I ride my motorcycle a bit and spend a lot of time in restaurants, but they don't know what it means to have responsibilities. I have to maintain my contacts continually, with the authorities, with my clients, and with the police. That takes a lot of time, money, and physical effort." That is also why he's fat, says Yingmin. "I'm not fat because I eat a lot; I'm fat because I drink a lot. I drink all the time with executives, people who are important for me. Drinking is very important for them. I don't care about it, but I have no choice. Formerly the party officers were fat; now it's the contractors who entertain the executives. Only the peasants and the workers are thin."

But for Yingmin it is not a wasted effort. Without the approval and the cooperation of the authorities, he would never have been able to realize his plan for his latest initiative, building migrant quarters. Yingmin believes that there is an opportunity since there is a shortage of sleeping quarters in Shenzhen for new and still-penniless migrants. "Most peasant workers are housed in tents.

That's how I started, too." Yingmin feels that he offers new workers "more decent" accommodations with the special quarters for migrants. Eight of them sleep in each unit and share the rent. They have to build the beds themselves, and it's not more than a concrete space.

Yingmin dreams about creating housing everywhere in Shenzhen for newly arrived migrant workers. He has persuaded himself that he'll do some good for the peasants and for society in this way. "I give these workers a permanent address and satisfy the employers. After all, there is a large turnover among the workers. They disappear from one day to the next, and that is usually related to the lack of stability in their personal lives. They don't have a fixed place of residence. Moreover, away from your family and your land, work is sometimes lonely. I know all about that. I think like a peasant because I've been a peasant; and because I've been here for such a long time, I understand what is needed."

A DOOR TO LIE DOWN ON

It was three o'clock in the afternoon when it started. The rain clouds were packed together so closely that it turned pitch-black in broad daylight. Rain started to fall from the sky in buckets, and in no time there was a four-inch-deep stream coming down from the hills. It was a miracle that the brick workers' quarters remained standing.

Children were crying, the lights had gone out, and the candles that were being used illuminated the worried faces of the peasant workers. They kept looking up at the corrugated metal roof on which the rain splashed down with a terrific racket. People had so often said *"Meishi,"* "It's nothing," that no one seemed to believe it anymore.

But nothing happened. Only the belongings of Yang Aiguo and four other peasants were soaked. The tent of the electrician employed by Wang Yingmin had blown away, and all his possessions had fallen victim to the wet fury. "This is my favorite book," says Aiguo with a glum smile. He places the soaking wet bundle of paper next to the lukewarm light of a fluorescent lamp. The book is about cultivating mushrooms. On the drenched pages are drawings of boletus and other fungi, and lots of heavy red underlinings and notes. In his free time Aiguo has been studying hard.

The boyish Aiguo—he is twenty-three years old, of small build, and full of energy—is a go-getter. He is from Longbeixiang in Sichuan, and, like many of his fellow villagers, he started in the city as a garbageman on a mountain of trash. That was dirty, unhealthy, and heavy work, and that's why he did it for only a year and a half, just until he had saved enough money to pay for training as a plumber and electrician. "I didn't want to stay on that garbage heap my whole life."

Back home in Sichuan he passed the training with flying colors, but the job to which he was assigned—a practice still customary at the time—was so little to his liking that he decided to pack his bags a second time. "I earned only 400 yuan [$49] per month. That was less than for collecting garbage!"

Fellow villagers who had been there made his heart beat faster when they told him about Shenzhen. Life in such a modern city near the border with exotic Hong Kong seemed like a good idea. An uncle introduced him to Wang Yingmin, and that's how he had landed here.

When I meet Aiguo, he is joining the rafters for the roof of one of the new migrant quarters that were being built on Yingmin's orders. Aiguo is balanced on the wall, which is as thick as a fist, and is busy with the narrow rafters. The structure looks extraordinarily rickety. The window frames and the doors are from the demolition yard; the masonry in which they are being placed has barely hardened; and the joints of the roof are attached to the walls with such thin clamps that a good storm would easily blow it back off.

Aiguo and his colleagues continue working hard because the unfinished space, which is only half covered by a roof, serves temporarily as the emergency accommodation for the men who were flooded out of their tent the day before. And the clouds above the city are again massing together ominously. The more roof covering, the more shelter later.

The men hoist up the sheets of corrugated metal, lug sand, level the ground, and finally make improvised beds: brick legs on which they place a door.

Just when Aiguo has finished, Yingmin shows up. For a moment he plays the boss, which he is, examines the structure of which he is the "architect," and hands over a stack of forms with new orders.

There is storm damage in a housing complex adjacent to Yingmin's construction site, and to remain on good terms with his neighbors, he lets them use his services free of charge. Aiguo and Wang Guanghui, Yingmin's older brother, are sent off with a can of waterproof paint, a roll of wire mesh, some brushes, and some tools.

On the ground floor in one of the complex's apartment buildings, a drainpipe has collapsed, flooding the whole basement. Without hesitation, Aiguo gets on his knees and to Guanghui's horror gropes with his bare arm in the stinking gunk where the drain is supposed to be. "I've never done such disgusting work," Guanghui says, gagging. Working on the land is one thing, but groping in someone else's filth goes too far. He prefers to remain at a distance.

But the fact that Yingmin, the boss of the business for which he is now working, is his brother, does not mean that he is spared. He has to do the work, too. "I used to work in a lamp factory," says Guanghui. "I earned 2,000 yuan [$248] per month, but there was no future in it. And it was boring work." That's why he called on his brother and came to Shenzhen. He has been there one month.

"I have to earn my success, just like everyone here. That's what Yingmin did, too. It's a question of time; he's been at it longer. I dream of my own business. Perhaps Yingmin will give me a real opportunity one day." He sounds unsure, but he ascribes special qualities to himself that he thinks Yingmin could find useful. "My brother is good at finding and maintaining business contacts, but he loses track of the situation; he is disorganized. I'm the guy who has an overview." Meanwhile, Aiguo lies on his stomach. His whole shirt is filthy, but that doesn't bother him. "I'll just wash it," he says cheerfully. Guanghui remains standing; he doesn't like to get dirty. He is wearing a dark blue suit that he's being careful with. Halfheartedly he uses a broomstick to poke in the steaming hole, but that has no effect either. The men decide to give up; they can't solve the problem, so they leave the bewildered inhabitants of the building behind.

Aiguo is still holding a stack of forms listing other buildings where there are leaks. The men climb on roofs, scrape out the cracks of concrete parts, spread some filler into them, and stick lengths of wire mesh over them—supposedly for strength. Aiguo does the work; Guanghui makes comments and hands him the materials. Close to seven o'clock they are finished and walk back to Yingmin's construction site.

The other workers have already begun to prepare the evening meal. Together with his half-drowned colleagues, Aiguo quickly takes a moment to complete that night's shelter. Everyone spreads his wet stuff out over wheelbarrows, scaffolding parts, and a concrete mixer. Aiguo himself goes once more through his drenched possessions: a class book—wet pages filled with poems and good wishes from former classmates—a smeared photo of the exam class, in which Aiguo, cheerful as ever, looks at the camera with a big smile, wearing a dark blue jacket and a pair of new shoes. "As a worker I need only one nice suit," he says while smoothing the jacket. Fortunately it's still dry. He doesn't have a *xifu*, a Western-style suit, which many of his peasant worker colleagues wear, because "suits don't look good on me. I'm too small for them."

Then Aiguo takes a quick bath. At least, he rubs his dry hair with shampoo. Then he fills an empty paint bucket with water. In a space within a forest of poles that support a just-cast concrete ceiling, he washes himself in the dark. Once he is dry and dressed, he combs a good-size dollop of hair cream through his hair. Aiguo even seems to be a bit vain. When putting on his nicest jacket, he asks one of the other peasants whether he's too thin.

Toward the end of the week Aiguo takes a bath. There is plenty of water. In the summer it falls from the sky in buckets. "If we could pour half of it over our fields at home, I would never have come here." Aiguo wonders why water falls from the sky exactly where it's least needed.

"I wear my nice clothes only when I go to Fuyong," he says. The center of Shenzhen's suburb is a large square where there is dancing in the evening. "I like to be there to look at people." He laughs. "I don't know how to dance, but I can see very well if someone else knows how."

Aiguo is not dissatisfied with his existence as a migrant worker. "Of course I don't want to stay in Shenzhen. Ultimately I want to go back home. But I think that being together with many young people is fine. I feel independent, and no one keeps a close eye on me. Once in a while I have to work hard, but after that my time is my own. Then I read or I go to Fuyong. I don't care how I live and where I sleep." Yet he longs for home. "I love Longbeixiang. That's where I belong. As soon as I have enough money, I'll go back. That will be in about three to five years. Then I'll start my own business." Aiguo wants to become a rabbit breeder or a mushroom grower. But there is another reason why he wants to go back: "In the city there's nothing to fall back on. If a factory closes its doors here, you're on the street, but at home I always have my land. I like that certainty."

During the years that Aiguo is in Shenzhen, he has to try to solve a "personal problem." That problem, Aiguo confesses, has to do with love. He has a girlfriend whom he would like to marry, but for this he needs money. And he doesn't have that by a long shot. Aiguo says that a marriage costs at least 10,000 yuan [$1,360]: enough for building a house, for purchasing the necessary furniture, and of course for the wedding.

But because of unforeseen circumstances, things didn't happen as he had planned. Aiguo's mother became ill, and so he has already returned to his village several times—out of concern and to see to it that the right decisions were made about the harvest. "You have only one mother, so I have no choice."

Yet he hopes to propose to his girlfriend this year "or at the latest next year." He has already asked her, but she hasn't given an answer yet. Keeping in touch is not easy. She works in a factory in Guangzhou, about sixty-two miles from Shenzhen, and he was able to call her only three times in the past year. Aiguo blushes when he speaks about his great love. "I'm not very good at writing letters," he says shyly.

Meanwhile it has become dark and the evening meal is ready: a watery tomato soup, fried eggplant, and rice. When one of the workers drops his bowl of food, everyone laughs loudly. The mood remains one of easy laughter. The men speak Sichuanese, and that is too bad for the only worker from Anhui. He is the one who doesn't laugh.

After dinner most of the peasants spend the rest of the evening doing laundry and watching television. The latter is an especially loved pastime; the small stools in front of the narrow cubicle where the television stands block the way far outside the door.

Aiguo goes to bed early, but his nightly rest can be called uncomfortable without any exaggeration. The wooden door that serves as a mattress is hard and narrow, and it is tolerable only if he lies on his back. Aiguo's advice: Never lie on your stomach, because that deprives your heart of the space for beating. It's unhealthy.

It is windy. The mosquito netting isn't closed properly, and everyone is beleaguered by the annoying buzzing insects. After some time it starts raining again, and the partial roof does not offer enough protection against the rain, which blows in. The clothes that are still hanging outside to dry become even wetter. The feet of the beds are exposed, but no one moves a muscle.

The men are sleeping, snoring loudly.

It is still raining the next morning, and an unspoken rule among the peasants says that they don't have to work. Aiguo pokes his head outside the mosquito netting, looks at the dark clouds above him, and pulls the blanket back over his head. He'll stay in bed for a while.

Yanhong shows not a trace of discomfort when she returns to her native village after many months. She still feels at home there, and her fellow villagers treat her as an old acquaintance, which she is. Everyone is proud of Shangdouyin's enterprising daughter, and Yanhong visibly enjoys the attention.

Embroidered Insoles

Those Who Stay Behind

(Hebei, Chicheng, Dongshanmiao, Shangdouyin)

Ganggang has caught a small hedgehog and together with his friends he is killing it. It is taking him all evening because it isn't easy to cut off the animal's spiny armor. His two friends lean practically on top of him while Ganggang does the work. He wields the knife, and with blood on his fingers he turns on a small oven to roast the dead animal.

It almost makes Li Yanhong puke. She can't understand her brother's investigative curiosity as he dissects the lifeless animal and studies its entrails as though he were a pathologist. "Yuck, Ganggang! Stop it!" she shouts angrily, and she pushes her younger brother with the hedgehog away out of the candlelight.

Li Yu and Zhang Yulian, the parents of Ganggang and Li Yanhong, grin from ear to ear. They are used to Ganggang's tricks. The boy is thirteen years old, and he keeps himself amused all day long in and around Shangdouyin. He no longer goes to school.

Suddenly Yanhong's parents seem ill at ease. They are ashamed not of their

Together with her grandmother, Yanhong visits her friends and relatives—just about everyone in the village. They all want to know how little Yanhong, now grown-up, is doing. They squeeze her cheeks and look her over approvingly.

son but of themselves. It is a mixture of embarrassment and pride, for Junior can't do anything wrong as far as his parents are concerned. But next to their independent daughter, who brings with her a whiff of the city—she goes to an evening high school in Beijing and works as a babysitter during the day— they are very self-conscious of their simplicity. You see them think how much Yanhong has changed.

Would Yanhong formerly have noticed the peasant shamelessness of the boy pouncing on his catch? And even though she is the pride and joy of the family, some of the enormous gap that she managed to bridge after leaving the countryside for the city has come between the parents and the daughter. Yanhong has become part of a world that those staying behind in Shang-douyin can only dream of.

• • •

The road from Beijing to Shangdouyin runs over one hundred miles of asphalt, gravel, and cobblestones. The trip takes six hours by car, although on
the Chinese scale the village is practically a stone's throw from the capital. But
it feels as if Shangdouyin is at the other side of the world. This village in Hebei
Province where the fertile soil of the coastal area and the dry, yellow earth of
the Gobi desert come together could on the face of it just as well be in central
Tibet. At this time of the year, the end of May, it is dry and barren. The colors
of the mud houses and the sandy lanes flow together seamlessly, and the bone-
dry dusty atmosphere that is especially characteristic of the villages in north
and west China give you the feeling of having traveled around the world when
arriving in Shangdouyin.

The almost six hundred inhabitants of the village experience this feeling in
reverse. For most of them, the voyage to a world where houses have window-
panes, where electricity and tap water are common, where toilets are more
than just a hole in the ground, and schools and hospitals are within everyone's
reach, is a giant undertaking.

The nine miles over the cobblestone path from the village to the closest
blacktop road are usually traversed on foot, unless the rickety bus that comes
at irregular times happens to come by. Then there is a long wait for a larger bus
along the regional road. But that bus stops only if the bus driver feels like it
and if he has no objections to the quantity of luggage the potential passengers
have brought along. It is only after several hours of reckless tearing over
mountain roads that causes people to gasp for breath that a larger city is
reached. From there a train chugs to Beijing in five hours. That journey is
made on straight, hard seats because comfort is hard to find on local routes.
Besides, there wouldn't be a peasant who would spend his money on it.

Most of the older villagers avoid that ordeal and limit their excursions to
those of the utmost necessity. They prefer to stay in Shangdouyin, which is
largely untouched by the stormy changes that are spreading in China's cities.

When Yanhong's father, fifty-year-old Li Yu, talks about Shangdouyin, the village where he was born and where his father and grandfather worked the same soil, he remembers the greatest change that took place at the end of the 1970s. At that time the Communist brigade of Shangdouyin was abolished. "Before that time we were a little bit hungry all year long," says the elder Li. His modesty makes it clear that he does not exaggerate. "Every year we were short two months of food. There was simply not enough food left for the whole village," he says. The reason for this was the defect that finally finished off the communes everywhere in China: None of the workers—Li's brigade consisted of thirty-five families—really did their best. "Diligence was not rewarded," Li explains of the reluctance among the peasants. In the end it meant the loss of one of the Communist pillars of Maoist China.

After 1978 the peasants of Shangdouyin were allowed to work for themselves for the first time since the 1950s, and this yielded a miraculous increase in production. "As if we had done nothing all those preceding years," says Li. "We were exhausted, but finally we had enough to eat once again." Yet the euphoria of those first months, when the Chinese peasants were allowed to trade their products in small amounts on the free market, didn't last long. For, as is always the case on the land, life was above all determined by the weather, and for years there has been a great drought in this part of China. "The soil is much drier than formerly," says Li.

During the past few years, this problem has worsened. Li explains: In Shangdouyin the soil is still relatively fertile, and many farmers who work the drier slopes have moved to the village over the years. "They have cultivated land in the surrounding mountains. That is a lot of work, while the yield is not large." This is why much of that just-reclaimed land now lies fallow again, which causes more slopes to erode, while the groundwater is retained for a shorter time. Moreover, observes Li as he stares at the sky, it rains much less than it used to.

The peasants of Shangdouyin work an average of 4 *mu*, or 0.66 acre. By Chinese standards, that is a reasonable amount, but a generation earlier Li's father still worked double the amount of acreage. On the other hand, Li says, today's farmers produce much more on the same piece of soil than in the past. Most farmers grow potatoes, millet, and corn. Old Li's land yields him 880 pounds of millet per year. Just like all other farmers, he has to hand over 22 pounds of it to the state as a tax.

The rest of the harvest is for the peasants' own consumption and for sale on the open market. But almost no one sells their produce anymore. The price of grain is exceptionally low, and everyone is waiting for a better offer. For some variety in their diet, the peasants of Shangdouyin trade by barter, which is flourishing. Li explains that this is done with the help of middlemen. They trade 2.5 *jin* (2.8 pounds) of millet for a pound of rice. For the time being, Li is keeping his stock untouched in storage while waiting for better prices in the summer, when demand is great.

For several days the peasants of Shangdouyin have had to do without electricity. Old cables are being replaced, and by order of the district administration, the current has been turned off so workers can complete the job safely.

It is therefore all the more striking when the amplified voice of the village chief sounds during the night. The public address system of the village committee sounds like old times, loud and indistinct. Once in a while it is used to call on villagers to report voluntarily for the installation of the new network. The committee has control of the key that gives access to the main switch and a backup power unit.

The arrival of the electricians with their impressive crampons that enable them to climb the newly installed concrete poles creates a lot of excitement in the usually humdrum life of the village. The work had been announced long ago, but after an official silence of many months, no one had counted on it any longer. Then a team of enormous-looking, unwashed, unshaved men in dented buses, run-down jeeps, and chugging trucks entered the village like a grubby circus parade. This meant that the villagers had to put aside their daily activities from one day to the next in order to fulfill their peasant obligation—electricity is for everyone—in the interest of the community.

Zhang Shiming, the treasurer of the village committee, mentions that each of the hundred families in the village is expected to cough up 200 yuan ($25) and lend a family member for a day's unpaid work. He has already gone door-to-door throughout the village to ask for help, but not everyone feels called upon to work. "Some come; some don't come; it can't be helped," Zhang says, resigned. He can't force anyone; times have changed. But if the installation of the new cables takes longer than was estimated by the district administration, the extra time is charged to the village. "In the end we are dependent on the effort of others." That is also true for other community projects such as repair work after flooding or for the construction of a new road. "Nothing happens without volunteers."

Fortunately, enough of the peasants are helpful, and people work steadily every day. Deep holes are dug for the concrete posts, and around the village center the scarce trees, mostly poplars, are cut down, provoking a lot of criticism. They are needed as wooden supports for the new posts. Men tug at heavy black cables with all their might, spurring themselves on with "One, two, three, pull!" All the activity is closely watched by a troop of pumpkinseed-chewing children who enliven these unusual events in their usually quiet village with much talk and happy chatter.

According to Yanhong, Li's daughter, who happens to be in Shangdouyin, nowadays such commotion is unusual. "Much more used to go on in the village," she says. "The children used to play more; the villagers did more things together." During the summer, Shangdouyin would regularly be visited by a touring opera company. Yanhong shows the run-down open-air theater, three cement walls with a roof and a red star in the middle of the ridge beam. Nowadays it serves as a grain and wood storage depot. The building looks abandoned, in the way that everywhere in rural China the community places of olden days have fallen out of fashion and into disrepair. On the crumbling

The party committee of Shangdouyin, gathered on the new treasure of the village: the electrical cable. When it is finally installed, the entire village will have power for the first time. According to Tian Ruihai (seated, center), the party secretary, the village will have to bleed collectively for this leap forward. "Nothing happens without volunteers."

stucco the soot spots from the wall candles that must have illuminated the makeup mirrors of the touring opera stars were still visible.

Yanhong still remembers seeing the villagers sitting on the small square in front of the building on their low, small stools, slurping tea, spitting, bustling about, and looking forward to the upcoming show. "That was a pleasant time," she says, melancholy. For her, Shangdouyin isn't what it used to be. "Formerly the village looked cleaner and better kept." It was alive.

This was also true for the small school on the other side of the square. Three years ago it was closed on orders of the district administration. The students moved to another school, outside the village. "As if the blood is slowly draining from the village. People no longer care about it," says Yanhong.

Nothing produces as much commotion in Shangdouyin as "the road," though. The road is a lifeline for renewal. The road would save Shangdouyin from decline. But all that connects Shangdouyin with the outside world is a meandering bed of stones, nine miles of tire- and stomach-stressing bumps before the saving asphalt of the closest regional street is reached. "Oh, the road," grumbles Tian Ruihai. He is the village party chairman—every community in China has a party chairman—and in rank he is higher than the village head. In theory his word has overriding weight, but in practice it is different. For years he has been working hard to get the road surfaced, but without result. Ask the villagers why Shangdouyin lags behind in the developments that have spread to other parts of the country, and all of them blame first the party officials and then the road.

"If I had known that it would be so difficult, I would never have sought election," says Tian, who combines his chairmanship with his work on the land. Tian knows that without a paved road, Shangdouyin's products won't reach the market, and no entrepreneur will dream of investing in the village. "But try and explain that to the village administration."

Several times the party chairman, the village head, and the treasurer have taken the hated cobblestone path to Dongshanmiao, where the *xiang* (district) administration has its seat, to argue personally to the administration members in favor of paving the road. They invited the party officials to dinner, drank countless glasses of *baijiu* (sorghum liquor) with them, one time even handed them a filled envelope, stayed overnight an extra night to rehash the affair the next day, and parted with vague—but they assumed sincere—promises. In the end it didn't help at all. Three times the men returned home empty-handed. Chairman Tian controls a snort, and his round face turns as red as the Chinese flag that hangs behind him. "Do you know what they told me the last time? 'Go back home. You are poor. That road, that's a waste of money. You won't know what to do with it.' What do you think of that?! In that way we won't get anywhere!" he says angrily. "It's a downward spiral," the chairman declares glumly about Shangdouyin's prospects. The village is doomed.

In all of Shangdouyin there is not a single person who still has faith in the high-ranking bureaucrats and party officials. If the peasants can be believed, the local party bosses are the dregs of society. "A bunch of corrupt bloodsuckers," sneer the residents. "Perhaps half of all the money that the central government allocated for the construction of a road was left when the money reached its destination," says chairman Tian.

The village committee is sure that it was not the fault of the party leaders in Beijing. The level of trust in the central government is unbelievably high. That is perhaps the most important reason why so little changes in rural China. The lower-level officials are the ones who get the blame. "The central government certainly spends money. We know that from the television. No one can prove that so much money is embezzled at the lower levels, but we see damned little of it back," Tian says angrily.

Many villagers agree with that. They trust their own people; after all, they have chosen the village committee themselves, and in their daily lives the party secretary, the village head, the treasurer, and the only policeman in the village are peasants and therefore fellow sufferers. "Those are not honorary posts," says Li Yu. "It's thankless work." They earn practically nothing for it—about 8 yuan per person per month, and this has to be raised by the villagers themselves. ("That makes them extra-reliable," say the villagers.) In addition, they waste a lot of time waging a hopeless struggle against the higher authorities.

It wasn't until 1997 that Shangdouyin went downhill rapidly. That year it was officially decided to reorganize the districts administratively, and the municipal administration that had until then been in Shangdouyin was moved to Dongshanmiao, located a distance away.

Because of the departure of the small army of officials, Shangdouyin also lost its high school and the prospect of new economic developments. The officials were willing to put in effort and hard work for themselves and their own children for projects from which the rest of the village could profit as well. But once they left, they took their plans with them.

The town council's move was far from subtle. For example, everything in the school building, which had after all been built with community money (in 1992 all the villagers spent 45 yuan, or $5.60, of their income on it), that could possibly be moved was taken along. "They took the glass panes out of the window frames and even took the doors along!" says Zhi Cungen, the village head. But villagers who cut bricks from the now worthless building received a fine of 2,000 yuan ($248). "But that building is ours," says Zhi, indignant.

Now that the school in Shangdouyin is closed, the children from the twelve villages that were served by the school have to go to the large district school in Dongshanmiao. But that turns out to be a big problem. Right after the start of the new school year in Dongshanmiao, the former pupils of the Shangdouyin school returned home by the dozen. They didn't want to go to their new school any longer. What was the problem? The peasants' sons and daughters who were now forced to stay in their new school during the week—Dongshanmiao is not easily reached from most of the villages around Shangdouyin—were afraid.

A local gang of eighteen-year-old bored, unemployed, recent graduates had made their lives thoroughly miserable. They cheated them out of their pocket money, stole their possessions, called everyone names, and used violence if they didn't get their way.

"They came only in the evening, in the school dormitories," says Ganggang, Yanhong's thirteen-year-old brother. He himself was harassed more than once, and every time the threats resulted in bruises and the loss of all his meager possessions. Finally Ganggang became so scared that he no longer dared to go to school. "They bother only the children whose parents live far away," says Ganggang.

Most of the children from the villages around Shangdouyin stay home. "The police do nothing," says Zhi, the village head. His son is one of those who no longer dare to go to school; he now helps in the fields. In the whole village only two children still go to school. "But they have relatives who work in the village administration," says Zhi. They are not harassed.

The worried parents spoke with the principal several times, but he did nothing. He too had school-age children, and he feared that they would take the rap if he took a stand against the gang. The villagers of Shangdouyin suspect that the Dongshanmiao police are cooperating with the gang members and let them harass the schoolchildren in exchange for a part of the loot. The result is that almost all children here steer clear of school and help their parents in the fields, look for work in the city, or, like Ganggang, hang around in the village all day.

More than 100 of the 556 registered inhabitants of Shangdouyin have left the village to seek their fortunes elsewhere. They are the peasants' sons and daughters who no longer believe that change will happen in the village— young women like Yanhong. They are the hope of those who stay behind. It is uncertain if they will ever return to the village, but it is all the same to their parents. "Of course we like to see our children leave," says Li Yu, Yanhong's father. Not one of the parents shows any sign of selfishness or possessiveness. Tradition plays no role at all for the peasants. No peasant father or mother would be proud if their son or daughter stayed behind in the countryside. That would indicate failure—for who would want a future without prospects for their child?

"The farmers influence one another. Sons and daughters who distinguish themselves are an example for those who stay behind and who will in the end also want to leave," says Li. Yanhong agrees. The few times that she visits her parents, she throws around her newly gained modest wealth. Her job in the capital as babysitter for a family from Europe earns her more money in a month than her parents can scrape together in a year. And the precooked chicken, the bags with fruit, instant coffee, cola, chocolate bars, jeans, athletic shoes, and lipstick that she brings for her family prove that.

Her parents sample these items without showing excitement—it all means very little to them. But that's not the purpose of the display. In her parents' eyes, Yanhong has broken away from the land. And although they understand little of the world in which their daughter has started a new life, they are proud of it.

"They're content with what they have," is the way Yanhong explains her parents' lives without ambition. Their house consists of two areas with paper windows, stone beds that during the winter are heated by wood-fired stoves at the entrance, a stable area, and an adjoining toilet—a ditch with two wooden planks lying across it. During the thirty years that they have lived there, little has changed. They have no running water and no central heating, seldom change clothes, wash themselves once a week (not at all in the winter), and are content with little variation in their lives. "And they never complain. They've been living for years in their way, and they stick to that," says Yanhong. That is true for most farmers. "Perhaps that's why so little changes in the countryside," she says tentatively.

In the evening she packs her bags. The next morning she will return to the capital, back to the future. Her mother prepares a bag with oats and lays out a pair of hand-embroidered insoles—the only things that she can think of to help Yanhong in the city. Yanhong immediately puts the insoles inside her black city boots. In this way she always carries with her a bit of her peasant past—in her shoes.

Li Yu's Account Book for the September 2000–September 2001 Harvest Year	
Income	
1,875 pounds beans ($0.06 per pound)	
2,200 pounds potatoes ($0.02 per pound)	
2,200 pounds Chinese cabbage ($0.002 per pound)	
770 pounds millet	
	Total: 700 yuan
Sale of 2 sheep (from his total livestock of	
10 sheep, 1 cow, and 1 horse)	500 yuan
Work/jobs (*dagong*) in construction and road building	1,000 yuan
	2,200 yuan
	($220.00)
Expenses	
Putting sheep out to board with the shepherd	
(at 35 yuan per sheep per year)	350 yuan
Manure	150 yuan
Seed	150 yuan
Pesticides	100 yuan
Agricultural tax (*zhongdishui*): state/district/village	
(12.5% of income—abolished in 2004)	260 yuan
Cost of living (oil/cigarettes)	800 yuan
Coal	300 yuan
	2,110 yuan
	($209.90)

撕

Tiny Plots of Land

Poverty
(Guizhou, Puding, Ganbacun)

There is a joke about China's poorest province: A peasant from Guizhou has eleven plots of land. After a day's work in the broiling sun, he counts his small parcels of plowed field. But he doesn't get past ten. Worried, he looks around and counts once again. Then, to his great relief, he discovers the eleventh parcel: It was covered by his straw hat.

Nowhere in China is there as great a shortage of arable soil as in Guizhou. Out of the 36 million people who live there, millions of farmers live on the edge of subsistence, and the most important reason for this is a lack of land. Because of the explosive growth of the Chinese population, this problem has become increasingly acute.

Eighty percent of the soil surface of Guizhou, which ironically means "valuable land," consists of hard, rocky soil. The karst mountains, which look like a child's drawing because of their cone shapes, are covered by a thin layer of soil. Only where the valleys are deeper and the soil layer thicker do the farmers work the land, tiny parcels that can be plowed in two or three steps—a good reason for those farmers who can afford it to leave the land. There is a steady population outflow from Guizhou.

What is happening in Guizhou on a small scale is taking place all over the Chinese hinterland. Because of overpopulation and a chronic lack of agricultural land, the peasants are leaving the countryside en masse. If there were fewer Chinese, the need to migrate would not be as great.

According to the latest population census of November 2000, there are 1.29 billion Chinese, of whom 851 million are registered as peasants. All the Chinese, with 22 percent of the world population, use no more than 8 percent of China's arable land. During the past decade, more than 70 million peasants have most likely lost their land to forced or illegal annexation by "local real estate developers," according to an estimate by Qin Hui, an agricultural expert at Qinghua University in Beijing. An additional 2 million peasants continue to lose their land annually. According to the Ministry of Agriculture, every year more than 328,600 acres of farmland are lost to nonagricultural use. All this repurposing creates great economic and demographic tensions.

A lack of land means a lack of income. In addition, the influence of China's rigid grain policy, which forbids grain trade on the free market, and the price competition from imports because of China's entry into the World Trade Organization (WTO) have caused the income of many farmers to decrease steadily in recent years.

Yet Chinese statistics report an increase in farmers' incomes every year. In 2004 it averaged 2,849 yuan ($353) per year, slightly more than the year before. But the peasants hardly notice it; instead they have seen their income evaporate every year—even before they have the cash in hand. Their paltry harvest yields less and less, and what they do earn has for years been disappearing in the form of taxes into the coffers of the district administration. The latter contends with a civil service that is much too large, budgets that are much too limited, and large debts. Until 2005, at least $75 billion in debt was created at the village and township levels.

The statistics don't take this into account. Instead they show that there is no country in the underdeveloped world where the problem of poverty is as small as in China. Indeed, if we were to believe the Chinese government, there is practically no poverty in China any longer.

In the autumn of 2000, the six-year campaign to wipe out all poverty in China came to an end. The Chinese government spoke of a great victory. In 1994, 80 million peasants were supposedly living below the subsistence level of 635 yuan ($78) per year, or 1.75 yuan ($0.21) per day. But six years later, according to the triumphant announcement of Chinese party leaders, the percentage of poor had decreased to under 3 percent, much less than the 12.7 percent in the United States or the almost 40 percent in the Philippines. The fact that this still involved 26 million people made no difference, according to the government. It concerned "handicapped" or "people who live under very difficult conditions."

It seemed an unlikely victory. Anyone traveling through China realizes that the problem of poverty must be much more widespread than the Chinese government makes it appear. The 26 million poor in a population of almost 1.3 billion should almost be swallowed up into the great mass, but that turns out not to be the case. The Communist Party is no doubt responsible for the fact that relatively few Chinese die of hunger, but their poverty is certainly visible.

According to the World Bank, the number of Chinese living below the poverty level is much greater. The World Bank uses a higher standard for the lower limit of the subsistence level, US $1 (about 8 yuan) per day, and has calculated that in September 2000, right before the end of the Chinese antipoverty campaign, 106 million Chinese, about 11 percent of the population, were living under that minimum. And 2003 was the first year since 1978 that the Chinese Bureau for Statistics reported an increase in poverty. Intuitively that seems to be correct. Chinese peasants with a total lack of financial means can be found everywhere. Those are the people without funds to buy the most vital necessities: a doctor's visit, new clothes, a warm blanket, or school tuition.

•   •   •

In Ganbacun, a village of the Buyi minority in one of the poorest districts of Puding in Guizhou, poverty is very apparent. There is a lack of just about everything: too little sowing seed; insufficient water to irrigate the fields; no electricity; and depending on the weather (usually it's too dry), there is starvation.

The antipoverty campaign never reached Ganbacun, and the population is left completely to its own devices. Village head Wang Busong, a sturdy man with bushy black eyebrows, has himself started a "nongovernmental organization to fight poverty." "I try to keep in touch with former pupils who have left for the city. In that way I hope that the village can make use of their knowledge," says Wang, who also teaches in the village school.

One-third of Ganbacun grows insufficient food to support itself, and Wang believes that with the help of modern agricultural techniques, more could be harvested from the arid soil.

On some of the wooden doors, reddish gold stickers have been affixed that show how many "stars" the inhabitants have earned. They indicate whether the peasants have a police record, whether they have paid all sorts of levies, and whether they have satisfied the family-planning requirements. The stars are meant as encouragement from the government, but they don't alter the discontent of many inhabitants.

A sixty-year-old woman farmer whose harvest was lost because of the persistent drought had to sell her stock of peanuts on the market to satisfy her tax obligation, which was in force in that area until 2006. And because in Ganbacun the tax had to be paid entirely in kind, she was forced to buy rice with the money she had earned and then turn that over to the state. She didn't protest. "It's useless," she said. But she does complain about it. Her opinion— "That's the way it is"—is widespread in this area.

Not all the peasants in Guizhou are as resigned. In Tongren and Kaili, two medium-large cities in the eastern part of the province, thousands of peasants took to the streets as early as the mid-1990s to protest against taxes and to demand attention for their hopeless situation. The army restored order, but the

Chinese authorities had a good fright. In the years that followed, larger and smaller peasant protests broke out all over the province. The government had been warned; the patience of the poor peasants was not infinite.

NOTHING BUT GOOD FROM XIAOGANG (Anhui, Xiaogang)

Although Xiaogang lies in a more favorable part of China, the peasants' problems there are almost the same as those of the peasants in Guizhou. The village has regularly had the personal attention of the country's most senior political leaders, but still it looks dilapidated. On feast days, say the villagers, you can see hundreds of party executives stroll up and down the only village's street. But when the dust blown up by their armored Audis has settled, Xiaogang, the center of the poor agricultural province, is again the quiet and neglected village it has always been.

Yet Xiaogang is a place where there was a revolution—hence the political bigwigs' interest. In 1978 eighteen peasants, against the Communist Party's policy, decided in secret to split up their commune. It was a contrarevolutionary decision, but according to Yan Hongchang, the now forty-eight-year-old plan initiator, it was the only way to end the catastrophic poverty and famine that the commune system had brought about. "None of us had the energy any longer to work the land. Whatever we did, there was never enough food for everyone."

The local administration protested, but Xiaogang soon obtained the approval of Wan Li, the provincial party secretary at the time. Within a short time the experiment of Yan and the other farmers became known all over China, and everywhere in the country the hated communes disappeared. It was the most important step in the direction of modern, market-oriented China—an event that is described in China as the "second liberation" (after that of 1949, the year of the establishment of the People's Republic).

But in Xiaogang things never got much beyond that historic change. The peasants live in better houses and still cultivate their own plots of land. They are no longer starving, but the rapid developments that took place after the abolishment of the communes on the east coast of China definitely did not happen in Xiaogang. Despite the interest of senior leaders, concrete help in the form of investments failed to materialize. "Xiaogang is at the other side of the world," says Yan. "No one is truly interested in what is happening in this village."

In the past few years, the Chinese party leaders have regularly expressed their worries about the pace of development in the Chinese countryside. Prime Minister Wen Jiabao considers it his "central task" to speed up this development. After the People's Congress in March 2005, he said, "I may not be an economist, but I am deeply aware of the importance of agriculture and the farmer peasants for China." In 2006, he announced with much fanfare what seems to be a version of Franklin Roosevelt's New Deal: "a new socialist countryside." According to Prime Minister Wen, this was a plan of historic significance. With the complete abolishment of taxes for farmers, the peasants would, for the first time in their history, be freed from disproportionately heavy burdens. In addition, Wen promised a financial boost of $42 billion for the development of the hinterland—an increase of well over 14 percent compared to the previous year. (As a comparison, the defense expenses, also a government priority, rose that year by the same percentage, to $35 billion.) Prime Minister Wen said that since the coastal region was now flourishing, it was the peasants' turn.

The income of the peasants has lagged far behind that of the city dwellers. In 2004, the per capita income in the cities (9,119 yuan [$1,130]) was more than three times higher than in the countryside. The Chinese Academy of Social Sciences has determined that when qualitatively important services such as good education and reliable medical care are included in the calculation, the income in the city is seven times higher than in the countryside. The prominent economist Li Zhining believes that the gap is getting larger because, according to his calculation, the income of the peasants and the growing underclass in the cities is decreasing instead of increasing. In the first quarter of 2005, 45 percent of the national income went to the wealthiest 10 percent of the country. The poorest 10 percent had to get by with 1.4 percent of that income.

According to the Chinese government, this is an explosively dangerous situation. It is so dangerous that, in the words of President and Party Leader Hu Jintao, the economic growth and even the continued existence of the People's Republic will be at stake if nothing is done about it. If the purchasing power in the countryside—851 million potential customers—does not pick up, there will be insufficient potential markets for the industrial products that are made in the city. This will cause the already inefficient government industry to run into even more trouble. The number of jobless will increase even more, and the stability of the country will also be in danger, according to the party leadership.

But it involves even more than just the peasants' income. In the past two decades, the countryside has never been as turbulent as in the past few years. The party itself reports ten thousand "disturbances of the social order" per year. In 2005 there were supposedly eighty-seven thousand such disturbances— thirteen thousand more than in the previous year. The increase was huge, to put it mildly. In 1994 the party counted ten thousand "disturbances." Place names like Dongzhou, Huaxi, and Tashi, where thousands of peasants took to the streets to protest the illegal confiscation of land, have since become synonymous with protest. There are daily reports about protests by farmers who take to the streets out of dissatisfaction with the corruption of party bureaucrats, arbitrary levies, the confiscation of land, the state monopoly of the grain trade, dishonest village elections, and many other grievances.

A carefully documented *Study of Chinese Peasants* (translated into English as *Will the Boat Sink the Water? The Life of Chinese Peasants*) by the married couple Chen Guidi and Wu Chuntao, published in 2004, came as a bombshell. In their book the two authors describe in careful witness accounts a succession of scandals in which peasants continually ended up diametrically opposed to unreasonable, corrupt, or criminal officials. The outcomes of these conflicts were always decided to the peasants' disadvantage; some even paid for it with their lives.

Even in Beijing the book received due attention. Chen Xiwen of the Central Leading Group of Financial and Economic Affairs of the State Council has confirmed the scenario described in the book. He confessed to the *New York Times* that he had bought two copies of the book, one for home and one for work. "I believe that things are even worse in the countryside," he said about the book. But he immediately played down his remark, saying "If it were really that bad everywhere, the peasants would be protesting all the time." He tried to make careful distinctions.

In March of 2004, several months after the publication of the *Study of Chinese Peasants* and after 7 million copies had sold, the book was officially banned. It might cause too much unrest in the countryside, the government reasoned; the peasants were not ready for it.

The situation has not improved much in Xiaogang. In the village there is great exasperation at the Chinese grain policy, which was completely restructured by former prime minister Zhu Rongji when he came into office in 1998. The reason: corruption. In that same year, the National Accounting Bureau determined that $30 billion of the $79 billion of the loans granted to state grain bureaus in the previous six years had been "lost." This was money that the 2,800 local grain bureaus had to use for the purchase of grain at a price slightly higher than the market price. It was supposedly to help the peasants. But a good part of that budget seemed to have disappeared into the pockets of the grain bureau officials.

The peasants were not directly bothered by this. They preferred to sell their grain on the free market. Despite everything, prices were higher there, and middlemen, unlike the grain bureaus, came to the peasants to pick up the grain.

In 1998 the Chinese government abruptly put an end to that "free" system.

All grain trade, except that by the grain bureaus, was controlled, and the grain bureaus were completely responsible for any losses. Where the economy elsewhere in China became increasingly free, the grain market was again in the iron grip of the state.

This was a great setback for the peasants, who were suddenly deprived of the advantages of the free grain market. The grain bureaus paid a price that, according to the authorities, was supposed to be 5 or 7 percent above the old market price; but this offered too little extra income to the peasants. "We used to earn more. That's for sure. Grain is the only thing that we grow," says Yan. But even the formerly outspoken peasants of Xiaogang reluctantly approve of the new policy. Their reasoning: "The people have an opinion, but the only opinion that counts is that of the leaders."

Wang Congquan, the acting district head of Fengyang, which includes Xiaogang, has obviously learned his lesson. "The central government wants to protect the farmers," he says. That is why he understands the value of the grain policy and the traditional obsession of Beijing with grain as the key link in this policy. "The peasants can count on a steady income." But doesn't he know that everywhere in China, including in his own district, the peasants complain about the limitations that are imposed on them? And doesn't he know that the grain bureaus absconded with the peasants' incomes on a large scale? "No," lies Wang; he knows nothing about that.

Honest answers are difficult to get in Xiaogang, but that is no surprise. Just as in other parts of China, the local government is under constant suspicion of embezzlement and abuse of authority. Very little about this is public in Fengyang. "But everyone knows it," confirms an official from the city. Corruption is the people's number one enemy. Very few people have access to the district's accounting records, and officials can do what they want with their budgets. Despite the thirty-year extension of the right to lease for the farmers—after all, the land belongs to the state—corrupt officials buy out the peasants and, against the rules, lease the land to companies. The government wants to deal with this evil practice by better protection of land use. Some

Chinese economists feel that the peasants, just like city dwellers, should be able to trade their land for a price. In the cities, homeowners can't buy land, but they are in charge of their property. They can develop it commercially. Peasants should be able to negotiate *directly* with the companies that are interested in their land, without the interference of possibly corrupt officials who put the lion's share of the settlement money in their own pockets.

According to Chen Xiwen, the agriculture expert of the Chinese cabinet, there are strict laws against the confiscation of land, but, like so many other laws in China, they are not sufficiently obeyed. Most officials ignore all state regulations. They claim land and demand all sorts of surcharges—despite the fact that in the past three years the agricultural taxation (a maximum of 5 percent) has been eliminated in most provinces.

But acting district chief Wang from Fengyang relies on the support of the population. He has seldom heard dissatisfied noises from the farmers in Fengyang. Wang says that if there had been any, he would certainly have received them from the district complaint department. An inquiry to Li Wenquan, the head of the letter and complaint division that exists in every district in China, turns out to be fairly useless. Li, who has access to all mail and personal communications from those among the 640,000 district inhabitants who are dissatisfied, is as silent as the grave. He says it's for reasons of privacy.

FRYING FISH

Ni Shenghai, Father of Jianjun
With a cup and a pail of water, fifty-year-old Ni Shenghai attacks the drought. His wife pricks a hole in the dry soil and lets a seed slip from her fist, and Ni sprinkles water over it. The dusty soil swirls around them, but Ni continues working unperturbed in the hot spring sun: a hole, a seed, a cup of water, a hole, a seed, a cup of water. Bit by bit the whole field is done.

Ni Shenghai, father of Ni Jianjun

It is almost impossible to imagine that all that effort will pay. "It doesn't," says Ni in his rich-sounding nasal dialect. It doesn't seem to bother him. "What else can I do?" he says. His wife stops working for a moment; she laughs out loud. What an attitude, she seems to think. A farmer sows his field without thinking about profit and prosperity. He'll worry about that later. "It's unprofitable," Ni concludes. His wife is again pricking holes.

Ni is happy that two of his three sons have left Shangdouyin. "I don't want them to return," he says resolutely. He is proud of his oldest boy, Jianjun, who has completed a training course, and that is more than many a person around there can say. Since Jianjun's success, the pressure is off for Ni. He believes that life is less insecure with a child in the city. "If he earns good money, we'll certainly follow him to the city," he says. He laughs heartily at the thought because he hasn't discussed anything with his son. But he is sure that, in the end, all children want to help their parents financially.

Jianjun never sends him money, but as far as his father is concerned, that is not necessary. By leaving, Jianjun has lessened his father's heavy burden. "All peasant sons leave. Jianjun knows that we have little money. We are very grateful to him."

Ultimately, everyone will leave the countryside. "Only the poor, the mentally disturbed, and the childless will stay behind," says Ni. They are doomed to the soil that is too dry.

Ni Jianjun, Cook, Changping

"I want my own restaurant," threatens twenty-two-year-old Ni Jianjun. His first day of work in the kitchen of a large restaurant in Changping was also his last. Jianjun turned out not to be qualified for preparing fish. "But I had told that in advance to the chef," says Jianjun. He feels he was taken for a ride and has big worries because he is broke and can't find work.

Earning a livelihood in one of the best-running sectors of the country— the restaurant system—is uncertain. Eating out, a popular activity in China, usually offers the peasant migrants their first job in the city. In China, just as in the rest of the world, Chinese restaurants are the unofficial reception centers for many newcomers. Not only is the demand great for cooks, cooks' helpers, and servers, but the supply is also overwhelming. And that makes life difficult for people like Jianjun.

"They can fire you whenever they want," says Jianjun about the restaurant owners—and they do, as many others before him learned. Since he was eighteen, Jianjun has been working as a cook in Changping, and he can no longer count the times he has changed employers.

He has a cook's training and has not lived at home since he was sixteen. In that respect, he is an experienced migrant worker with more qualifications than many of his fellow villagers. But until now that has made no difference. "You have to call in at the restaurants like a beggar to offer your services," says Jianjun. "After that, if you're lucky, you can come and do trial cooking for a while." If you do it well, then you can stay. "One time I

Ni Jianjun

worked in a restaurant where I earned $120 per month; that was the best work I ever did." In addition to the salary, he received board and lodging: fried vegetables with white rice every day and three chairs from the restaurant to sleep on.

Sweat drips from his chubby face. He can't stand calling in at the restaurants. But he definitely does not want to go home. Shangdouyin has nothing to offer him. His independence is valuable to him, and he won't have that in the countryside. It is only with a steady job that he will perhaps one day meet a woman. "Nowadays no woman wants a man who lives off the land," he says. As soon as Jianjun has his own restaurant, he will let his parents come and join him. That's his plan.

Dezhe gets the news from the old papers that he collects. It makes no difference to him that it's old news, as long as there is something to read. Sometimes, when he watches television, he discovers that what he has just read was outdated long ago.

Garbage for a Living

Garbagemen

(Sichuan, Bazhong, Longbei, Mangzicun)

When Wang Hongmei realized that her son had run away from home, she cried for a week. She was fond of Chunming, and he cared about her, which was rare in the village. Her husband, Yang Baiming, who acted as if he wasn't worried, tried to reassure her—when the time was right, Chunming would let them hear from him. After all, the fourteen-year-old didn't have a red cent, and he had never been farther away than the bamboo hedges on the mountain ridges around the village; he would never be able to find his way.

But the days passed and no news was forthcoming. Hongmei was inconsolable. It was then that Baiming decided to look for his son.

Standing on a chair, he reached with one hand for the small metal box under the roof beam, gave it an approving smack, and blew off the dust. In that box he kept his savings—not much, but enough for a trip to the capital, since Baiming suspected that that's where his son was.

For the men and the boys in this village, Beijing was paradise, a city far from Mangzicun. From there to Beijing meant first thirty minutes of walking, then forty-five minutes by motorbike, one hour by minibus, four and a half hours on a big bus, and twenty-seven hours by train. Nothing could be better than

Beijing; that's what they all told one another. It had to be really great to live in the spot where the country's leaders had their homes.

Chunming had regularly expressed his wish to go to Beijing, and Baiming suddenly remembered how three days before his disappearance his son had been very pleasant and had asked his father all sorts of things about travel by train. Although Chunming usually didn't talk to his father and was more often grouchy than pleasant to him, that had not aroused any suspicion. Baiming had enjoyed it. The boy had never seen a train, and his interest seemed genuine. "He wanted to know how it went, travel by train," Baiming recounts, from buying a ticket to the long road to the nearest station. Unsuspecting, Baiming had told him everything. He could have kicked himself.

Baiming shook the tin box but heard nothing. His heart missed a beat. It was empty! The money that he had earned half a year ago in Xi'an and that he had wanted to use to buy a new plow was gone. He had been robbed. Now it was Hongmei's turn to kick herself—hadn't Chunming asked her that same week about his father's money? She had pointed out the secret spot to him! How could she have been so stupid? Of course Chunming had taken it! Her very own son had robbed them. Right away she started to cry again.

"He had a classmate bring his schoolbag home with the message that he was going to stay with another friend for a few days," remembers Hongmei. Going by the school to check whether that was true was not an option. "It's an hour's walk to the village, and I had to work." Three days later the teacher came by to see what was wrong with Chunming, and it wasn't until then that Hongmei knew for sure that something was up.

Upon inquiry in the village, it appeared that Chunming was not the only one who had run away. He had gone together with a friend, but the latter had turned around after two days. The boy had gambled away his money in Bazhong, after a seven-hour trip from Mangzicun. After a few days he came back to his worried parents, his tail between his legs and broke. Through him Baiming had found out about Chunming's plans: He was on his way to see an uncle by marriage, the former teacher Liu Dezhe who years ago had left the village and had become a garbageman in Beijing. The story went that he was none the worse for it, and in the meantime many fathers and sons had found their way from the village to the garbage dumps of the capital, in search of their own golden eggs.

In the end, Baiming borrowed the money for the trip to Beijing. During the uncomfortable train trip—he had bought the cheapest ticket and stood or sat on the floor for the entire twenty-seven hours—Baiming became very angry. If he found Chunming, he would teach him a lesson.

For a whole day, Baiming went around to the mountains of trash in east Beijing asking for his son, until someone answered in the affirmative. Chunming was indeed with Liu Dezhe. Once Baiming saw his son, who threw his arms around his father's neck, crying, all his anger ebbed away. Together they immediately called the post office of Mangzicun and passed the message to Hongmei that she no longer needed to worry. Her son had been found.

Chunming chuckles furtively. He still feels a little guilty. He is twenty-three years old now, an experienced migrant worker, but he can still remember his departure from Mangzicun as if it were yesterday. "I was sick and tired of the nagging about my school performance," he says apologetically. "I didn't do well at school. So what?" There were many boys of his age who hadn't finished junior high school. "I wanted to work, earn money, become rich. I knew people in Beijing." He had never been afraid. When his friend with whom he had run away gave up after two days, it took him a moment to get over it. But once on the train on the way to the capital, he felt strong. "There was no space anywhere in the train, but there was a nice man who let me sit on his knee." Because of that he had not aroused the suspicion of the conductors, for a child without a companion would most certainly be thrown off the train.

Halfway through the train trip, a man walking down the aisle called him loudly by name. Chunming had the scare of his life and thought that he had been caught. But it was a fellow villager who happened to be on the same train, a one in a thousand chance. The man befriended Chunming and took him to the place outside Beijing where Liu Dezhe and the other villagers from Mangzicun handled thousands of pounds of garbage daily.

Dezhe did not look happy when gangly Chunming walked into the improvised shelter of wooden pallets, flattened oilcans, and unfolded cardboard boxes. It seemed that half of Mangzicun had appealed to him during the past few years, and he was certainly not looking for clumsy, lazy teenagers.

But the boy's determination convinced him eventually, and he actually thought it was a good joke that a child of fourteen had traveled more than nineteen hundred miles to root in someone else's stinking trash. Chunming was allowed to stay, but he was not allowed to go up the garbage heap. He was made responsible for Dezhe's youngest child when both parents were going though garbage. In exchange, Dezhe gave him food and a roof over his head.

TROPHIES

It was not the towering apartment buildings, the endless lines of cars, the masses of people, the beltways, or the sporadic foreigners that made an impression on Chunming when he arrived in the capital. No, it was the immense quantity of smoldering and stinking garbage at Dezhe's collection point. "I never thought that a city like Beijing could produce that much filth," says Chunming. The television had never mentioned that. He simply thought that the capital was an oasis of luxury and progress. But around the thriving center of power lay islands of rotting trash. And the people who rooted in it like pigs, even his fellow villagers, seemed not to be bothered by it at all! "The first week I kept puking. But everyone said that that was normal. 'At a certain point you no longer smell it,' they said. And that was true." Chunming had not let him-

Often there is nothing to do. "As long as there is something to eat." Dezhe says that's the advantage of independent work. "Sometimes nothing is going right, but no one forces me to go to work." Such freedom outweighs a steady income in a factory.

self be chased away by it; he had come with a mission. He wanted to try his luck, and complaining was simply not done. "I wanted it myself."

In this way Chunming became a full-fledged member of the garbage colony. Day in and day out, forty of them would go through the contents of about one hundred large garbage trucks—with a steel hook in their right hand and a basket around their left shoulder. Styrofoam, bottles, cans, glass, cardboard—Chunming picked out everything that still had value and dexterously raked it into his basket. Sometimes he found radio or television parts, toys, cassette tapes, lamps, and chairs. After a few weeks of digging, Chunming concluded that the inhabitants of the capital were very wasteful. Just like the others, he used anything that had some worth to put together a household in his temporary cardboard accommodations. His bed was an old door, he

Dezhe's children have grown up among the trash from the city. He would have preferred other surroundings for them, but no matter how unattractive it is at times, "the future is here in the city."

plucked a table out of the trash for himself, and at the head of his bed stood a stereo system that he had cleverly put together from repaired parts that the former owners had discarded. And it worked!

It didn't take Chunming long to realize that his first job in the big city had few of the prospects that he had imagined so vividly before his departure from Mangzicun. All he had to do was look at his digging and slogging fellow villagers to realize that his fantasy was not very realistic. Most of them, like his uncle Dezhe, had been in Beijing for years, and they were still doing the same work. And to say that it had made them rich would be telling a lie. Chunming determined that most of them had not gotten any farther, never got beyond the garbage dump, and probably never would. "Everyone told me that getting better work was out of the question because you then have to compete with the city population," says Chunming. "Garbage was and is ours; no Beijing resident bothers with it, but as soon as there is interesting work, we stand no chance." The city resident always has preference. It seemed that with garbage work, everyone earned just enough to continue despite everything and still not want to return to Mangzicun.

This is also what happened initially to Chunming. He lived from garbage for more than seven years before deciding that his life had to change. His trophies from endless rooting had steadily increased—more cassette tapes, radio parts, comic books, teacups, and even a whole bicycle—but he had never found happiness and riches. "I was fed up," says Chunming.

It was a friend who suggested that he apply to the army. "He had done it for

When the photographer Liu Jingxing met Chunming for the first time in the early nineties, the latter didn't like the attention. "I didn't understand his interest," Chunming says later. When he sees himself again in that early photo, he is uninterested. It is a phase in his life that has no special meaning for him. Only the memory that he had escaped the village and his parents' home gives him a feeling of relief.

two years and was enthusiastic. I saw it as an opportunity to improve myself."
He was told that it would strengthen his self-respect, and that would be useful
in the future. "I had never had such a clear goal," says Chunming. In addition
it was a very patriotic goal.

When the news reached Chunming's father, he was not happy. He thought
it was a bad plan. Chunming would be wasting his time. He himself had
served eleven years in the military, but it hadn't gained him anything. On the
contrary, he had felt used. "Patriotism, forget it," he supposedly said angrily. A
well-disposed grandfather had been needed to win Baiming over so that he
would give Chunming the needed permission.

"Before I went into the army I was embarrassed to open my mouth. I've become more self-confident in the army," says Chunming. He served two years,
and photos show him proudly standing on a tank: the peasant boy from
Mangzicun who has become a soldier. He enjoyed his newly obtained status,
even though he was only a foot soldier and his day consisted of many useless
exercises and chores (the courtyard of the barracks where he was quartered
could not be swept often enough). But as a member of the People's Liberation
Army and participant in a proud Communist tradition, he had prestige in
China.

After two years of service, Chunming did have to admit that prestige was all
he had gained. "I thought that military service would help me along, but that
wasn't so." His superiors in the army had tried to have him sign on for more
time. "Yang, you're a good soldier," they said. But Chunming was no longer
convinced. He had accidentally discovered that one of his bosses had cheated
and had bought his position for 30,000 yuan ($3,720). No one had dared to re-
port it, even though it had been at the expense of his and his buddies' pay. But,
even more important, after two years of faithful service, he was still broke.
"You work yourself into a sweat for your superiors, for that's the only way
to get on. If you don't do that, you remain a foot soldier." And soldier Yang
hadn't felt like remaining one.

This photo of Chunming, taken by Jingxing, was in several army publications. "From Garbage Boy to Soldier" was a story that spoke to many people's imaginations. But Chunming hasn't missed the army at all since his discharge.

This is how Chunming came to pack his army things and beat a retreat. He went back to Uncle Dezhe in the capital. "I was set on staying in the city," says Chunming. "That's where the future is." Uncle Dezhe and the others were not surprised. He was greeted exuberantly, his uniform was admired, and finally Chunming felt appreciated.

UNCLE DEZHE

During the two years of Chunming's absence, it had become quiet on Dezhe's garbage dump. All the villagers were still there, but most of them kept busy chewing pumpkin seeds and watching television. The women knitted. There

After many years, Dezhe is used to improvising. Taking a bath is no luxury. You just do it outside with a small basin if the weather permits. And if not, as in the winter, then he simply doesn't wash himself.

was no work. The courtyard was practically empty, and the stinking mountain of garbage had shrunk to the grimy, sandy soil. What had happened to the flourishing business of urban trash?

The committee of the neighborhood where Dezhe used to process his garbage had without warning seized all his papers and declared the supply lines from and to the city illegal. It appeared that Dezhe had not complied with environmental regulations—supposedly it was too dirty. The peasants had been incredulous. "Too dirty?" Dezhe had shouted angrily. "Have you ever seen clean garbage?" But his anger had been to no avail. The garbage had to go and, if at all possible, Dezhe and his rag-picking friends as well. The garbage colony from Mangzicun was now awaiting the mercy of the neighborhood committee. To try to move the gentlemen to come to another decision—everyone was short of income, and no one had built up enough of a buffer to weather such a crisis for a long time—Dezhe had deployed heavy artillery. He had dipped deep into his fast-dwindling supply of money and had treated the committee to prostitutes. Dezhe tells it afterward as if it had been about a carton of cigarettes. Then he sniggers, "It wasn't cheap." But it hadn't helped. They had not yielded an inch.

The sudden diligence of the neighborhood committee—the members had never been difficult to bribe—was the result of an order of the city council of Beijing, which at that time was making frantic efforts to secure its candidacy for the 2008 Olympic Games. No Olympic inspector would ever think of inspecting Dezhe's collection point, but this time the neighborhood committee was totally serious and, according to Dezhe, saw "another chance to screw us."

In that light the neighborhood committee had also decided that the muddy alleys in the district where Dezhe piled his trash had to be cleaned. It had always been a mess, like all migrant districts on the outskirts of the capital—muddy, drab, and dirty. But in accordance with a vague municipal guideline, all the walls that bordered the alleys had to be repainted. Someone in the administration had the bright idea that the paint should be bright pink. Because of this, the grimy quarter right next to Beijing Steel, the stinking and puffing steel company that had caused many city inhabitants to have significant asthma, had changed into a bizarre landscape where everything was hidden under a thick layer of black carbon, except for the cotton candy pink walls.

Dezhe and the others were sick of the corruption and extortion that they had to put up with, but what could they do to counter it? "Protesting is for the Falun Gong," Dezhe had said. The outlawed religious movement had been in the news almost daily, and everyone could see what protesting could lead to. Even when the villagers hadn't done anything drastic, the police had in the past seized the residence permits of Dezhe or other villagers at regular intervals. These papers then were torn up, even if they were in order, and the men were put in an internment camp in Changping, outside the city, and then put on the train back to Mangzicun. In the end most of them returned, even though it cost a great deal of time and money.

But this time Dezhe had not taken into account the whims of the neighborhood committee. He thought that they were on his side. After all, he was no newcomer and had seen no danger when he had started his own business a few months earlier. He had put together 40,000 yuan ($4,960), money that he had saved with difficulty over the years, and had purchased the rights for the rent of a nearby abandoned factory, an empty square as large as half a football field with rectangular rooms at two sides, perfectly suited for his garbage-processing.

But the ink was barely dry on the agreement when the members of the neighborhood committee started their extortion campaign. They must have thought that someone who could put down 40,000 yuan must have some more resources. According to Dezhe, it was a setup; the previous renter had been in cahoots with the neighborhood committee and had tricked him into it.

Dezhe spends his many hours of involuntarily free time watching television on an old, discarded sofa in one of the bare rooms of his recently acquired factory. He has to support a family, and all the villagers who work for or with him, a total of thirty families, are waiting, idle and unemployed. How things will go, no one knows.

Dezhe thinks back with an unreal feeling of wistfulness to the time when he wasn't his own boss yet. Going back to his old workplace is no option because the situation there was intolerable. The way it happened was really too strange for words. Dezhe's young son had a fight with the son of his former boss. It was about nothing special, just a fight between kids, and the boys made up the next day. But the boys' mothers had meddled in it and were at each other's throats. It had been a real scene. Everyone had surrounded the quarreling women. Only the boss had remained at a distance. From that moment on, Dezhe and his boss no longer hit it off. "I wanted to get away. Start for myself and no longer be dependent on others," Dezhe says while he drowns away that bad memory with a big swig of gin.

When Dezhe left for Beijing in 1989 as one of the first from his village, he imagined the future very differently. The villagers thought he was a daredevil, a pioneer, but above all they admired him. Until that time Dezhe had been a teacher at an elementary school, but when he was twenty-five he abandoned it because of frustration with the Chinese education system. "I had one class with all ages," says Dezhe, who now is thirty-seven. "It was impossible. I couldn't give any child the attention he needed." Dezhe didn't dare to say anything about it and wrote an article that got into the local newspaper. But his classes remained jam-packed. After six difficult years and still as penniless as when he started, Dezhe decided to stop.

"In the countryside, prestige is determined by wealth, not by intellect," he says. Farming had never fascinated him, and he had passed up his right to land. "Your own land just costs money," he says.

His departure for Beijing was final. Dezhe never wanted to go back. "Beijing is the big brother," he says. He was jealous of the well-to-do people in the most beautiful city in the land, and he was willing to sacrifice everything to become part of it. "Everything is better in the city," he says, "except perhaps for the food."

The leap from the classroom to the garbage of the capital caused him no trouble at all. "I knew what I did it for. I was prepared to go much deeper through the mud." And he did, literally. Rummaging through the trash was not good for his health. The dust has choked his lungs, and like many of the garbagemen, Dezhe suffers from a skin disease. According to Dezhe, that is the risk of his work. Most of the trash workers and their children had diarrhea for a long time, until they got used to their unhygienic living and working environment. "In the long run it gets better. You become hardened."

But there is a self-imposed taboo on experimenting or playing with medical waste. "One time two friends and I found a bottle with transparent liquid. We thought that it was gin and took a big swig of it." But it turned out that it wasn't gin. Dezhe became ill, and his two drinking buddies, who had much more than he, didn't survive.

After twelve years of slaving away, Dezhe himself says that he has achieved little and has had to endure a lot. "I have come to dislike the inhabitants of the capital; they look down on us," he says. The residents of Beijing treat their peasant fellow countrymen with contempt all the time, and almost no one in the city is courteous or friendly to the migrants. Dezhe is very sensitive to that because as an educated peasant he often feels much smarter than the "locals." "I collect their trash, I contribute to the improvement of the environment," he says, choosing his words carefully, "but I feel treated like a dog. People here judge easily. I may look like a country bumpkin, but I'm not stupid." To prove it, he gives his opinion about the Communist Party, the Falun Gong, the Taiwan question, and recycling. "I can discuss current political events." Dezhe gets this information from the newspapers and magazines that he has found on the streets for many years.

And yet Dezhe wants to stay. He has a future here. It may be uncertain, but still, he knows that peasant life offers no prospect at all. From the whole time that he has worked in Beijing, Dezhe knows exactly one peasant who has been successful. "But," Dezhe explains away his own lack of success, "his wealth wasn't earned honestly; he was lucky." The man, an uncle of Chunming, had found 180,000 yuan ($22,320) in the trash. One hundred eighty thick stacks packed inside cigarette cartons. Dezhe suspects that the intended recipient of the money must have been a high-ranking executive who never discovered the discretely packaged request for a favor. "It was around the Chinese New Year, and at that time it is customary for corrupt lower-ranking executives to try and bribe or favorably dispose corrupt higher-ranking executives." The cigarette cartons were unopened and had perhaps landed in the garbage during a house cleaning. Dezhe chuckles. "The man didn't turn the money in to the police, as the law requires, but he immediately bought a house with it. I would have done that, too. His wife knew nothing until a realtor called and she picked up the telephone. Can you imagine? She was furious, but her spouse defended himself and said, 'If I had told you, the whole world would have known.' Of course he was right, for we all know it now."

STEPPING WITHOUT SPLASHING

It is almost Chinese New Year, and Chunming is getting ready to go home. He too participates in this yearly ritual of most migrant workers because it is an opportunity to deliver in person all the money earned in a year of hard work— and, last but not least, to see loved ones and friends again.

Only Dezhe remains behind in Beijing.

He finds the yearly trek "inconvenient" and says that he no longer has any business in Mangzicun. "The trip costs a lot of money and entails many obligations," he complains. The last time that he went home, years ago, it cost him two months' income. In the eyes of those who stayed behind in Mangzicun, Dezhe was experienced, rich, and influential, and wherever he was invited ("and I was often invited"), he left some money out of loyalty.

Chunming has to laugh at his uncle. He doesn't share the latter's worries because he has no money anyway. There is nothing to get from him. His return to Mangzicun is mainly the result of boredom and pragmatism. For days on end he sits chewing pits in front of the TV, but in Mangzicun he may run into classmates who might be able to help him find a job elsewhere in China, a job that earns more than collecting trash does. "I don't do anything for less than 1,000 yuan [$124]," threatens Chunming. Most garbagemen earn less, and that is why collecting garbage is a closed chapter for him.

Usually Dezhe skips Chinese New Year. But once in a while he does go—at his wife's urging. "I long for home. I've got to see everyone again," she says. Dezhe follows her, but reluctantly.

Since leaving the service, he has applied for jobs a few times, but every time without success. He has solicited perfunctorily at several companies, each time in response to an ad, but was turned down everywhere. "I said that I am prepared to learn and that they should fire me if I don't do it right. But the only thing they said was 'Don't waste your words, just leave.' Isn't that insulting? It makes me furious."

From time to time Chunming becomes despondent, even though he is seldom heard to complain. But it makes him lie awake at night. Then he thinks about his parents' home in Mangzicun and how his mother nags him with increasing frequency and asks him when he is finally getting married. "When I explain that I first want financial stability because I don't want to fall back on her and my father, she understands. But it doesn't stop her worries."

Yet Chunming has no doubt that he will sooner or later meet the woman of his dreams. The young man from Mangzicun has no work and no money, wears his uncle's clothes, and sleeps on a plank in a cardboard hut with two other people, but he has no lack of self-confidence. "I swear to you that in two years I'll be out of the woods," he says with such conviction that he must be right.

At home in Mangzicun, the huge houses on the densely built-up land of rice terraces and bamboo hedges reveal even from a great distance the economic ups and downs of Dezhe and Chunming's fellow villagers. If the façades are white, things are going well for the villagers, and at least one member of the family is sending money from outside the village. But if a façade almost fades into the sand-colored background, then the yield from the land is probably the only form of income, and there is poverty under the roof. In Mangzicun many houses are plastered white. Chunming thinks that more than two-thirds of the peasants have one or more family members who have left the land to work in the city.

This has caused an unparalleled demographic revolution in the village. The young men and women from Mangzicun, like Chunming, but more often also their fathers, work outside the home for the greatest part of the year. Young parents leave the care of their children to their mothers, while these same older women also have complete responsibility for working the land.

That is exactly why the weeks around Chinese New Year are so special. The families are together only once a year. That is when parents and children get together, classmates hold reunions, and villagers catch up on news. At that time there is a coming and going of friends and family members. People eat, drink a lot, and brag at length about the successes and losses in that other harsh world, far away from home.

Chunming returns from visits to an uncle, a cousin, the local party secretary, and a school friend. He is pretty drunk from the sugary-sweet gin, a local brew, but he still walks deftly across the narrow dikes along the rice terraces. It has rained all day, and the roads and the soil have dissolved into a big mud bath. But Chunming has an amazing talent for stepping without splashing. Even the trouser legs of his two-piece Western-cut suit—worn especially for the occasion so that those who have remained behind can see how citified he has become—are still blue and without mud stains. Where any other person would have taken a gigantic fall on the slippery soles of his city shoes, Chunming climbs effortlessly up the steepest muddy inclines.

"Do you understand now why I want to get away from here?" says Chunming. Despite his agility, traipsing over the flooded farmland really exasperates him. Pavement, or lack of it, was an important topic of conversation during every visit of the day. It is a trip that shouldn't take even half an hour if there were an asphalt road. But because the mountain path consists of nothing but mud and large cobblestones, the trip on a motorbike takes almost two hours. All migrant workers from the village have traveled the road home grumbling, and everyone still complains that almost no driver is willing to make the trip over the slippery, bumpy path. The traffic to and from Mangzicun is limited to one or two vehicles per day. And that limits development in the village considerably.

Hongmei, Chunming's mother, is beside herself with joy. The feigned un-interested and dissatisfied attitude of her son makes no impression on her. Her boy is home, her husband is back, and together with her eleven-year-old daughter she wants to celebrate. That means that the thickest piece of lard was taken down from the rafter, half of a smoked pig's head (for good luck) is chopped up in a pan, and white dough balls are deep-fried and rolled in melted sugar—a peasant meal that requires a strong stomach and is accompanied by quite a bit of sweet-gin drinking.

"Chunming is a good boy," Hongmei says during the feast. She has long ago forgiven him the fact that he ran away and emptied the family cashbox. "He didn't want to burden us any longer," says Hongmei sympathetically. Since that time, Chunming has brought in a steady stream of money—not much, but enough for his mother and his sister, Aimin, to get by. "Aimin has cost us a lot of money," says Hongmei. "If it hadn't been for Chunming, we would never have kept Aimin." Ten years ago, Hongmei found the little girl by the road. She was a month old at the time. Hongmei decided to take care of her. But after five months the family was fined because of a violation of the one-child policy. Eleven hundred pounds of rice and three pigs were impounded. "They threatened to tear down our house if we didn't pay. Then I tried to give away the baby, but Chunming began to cry. He didn't want to lose his new little sister." Aimin stayed, but the family never recovered from the financial setback.

No one counts on the income of Chunming's father any longer. Over the years Baiming's gentleness and reserve have gained the upper hand, which is why he stands up less and less for himself and his family. Recently, after a half year of diligent work in building in Xi'an, he accepted angrily but silently the fact that his boss refused to pay the promised wages of $484. "His brothers were like that, too," says Hongmei. "They never stood up for themselves. They couldn't do it." One of them swallowed some agricultural pesticide and put an end to his life.

Chunming can't stand to listen to these stories and leaves. He has hardly been a week in Mangzicun when he longs to go back to the city. "Not because I feel at home there," he says, "but what's the point of being here?" The gin has clearly gone to his head. He hasn't told anyone how miserable his situation actually is. "In Mangzicun the chances are limited to the land, a corrupt village administration, or the local village school."

An outsider gazes in admiration at the wonderful landscape, but Chunming is bored to death. He pretends to be annoyed at the primitive customs and the superstitions. At a pulled-down tombstone in the middle of the most important mountain path that leads to the main street, he laughs scornfully because all of Mangzicun would have feared that grave. "Cows and pigs were dying. Supposedly it was the fault of the district head who was buried in the grave. He was unpopular, and with his grave he supposedly cut off the most important energy fields to the valley. Then his tombstone was pulled down. Since then the qi should be streaming again. But the cows and the pigs are still dying."

Chunming avoids peasant society and its customs. The few weeks that he is home, he spends whole days in front of the grainy screen of a black-and-white television that he found and repaired at one time. Much of his time is spent brushing his city shoes, smoking cigarettes, and slapping his cold hands together to warm them.

"Every father wants his child to leave the land," says a great-uncle of Chunming. In Mangzicun there is no desire to continue peasant traditions. No one is proud of them. The land stands for decline; the city is the future. Chunming's great-uncle, like most of the peasants from the village, has earned his money as a garbageman in Beijing. After ten years of heavy work, a tolerance for city stench, and the torture of a skin allergy contracted there, he attained what he always dreamed of: His children, two sons of twenty and twenty-five, recently changed their peasant status for an identity card of a nearby city—an administrative transaction that is allowed at the provincial level.

The young men look the part. They are well fed and well dressed. Obviously they are of a different sort than the stay-behinds in Mangzicun, who are

Some villagers have waited all day to catch a ride on an empty truck.

without prospects. "In the end," says Chunming's great-uncle, "we all profit." The tile floor in his loam house, the video-CD player, the pink polyester blankets on the two-person bed, a water kettle, and a threshing machine in his farmyard—all these are the result of money from elsewhere. No wonder, then, that the façade of his peasant home is freshly plastered. It looks significantly whiter than those of the neighbors. Chunming can only dream of that.

毀

A Halfhearted Welcome

Rules
(Hebei, Dingxian, Dingzhou, Sibiancun)

The migrant's existence is filled with setbacks that are often so great and fundamental that it is difficult to understand what moves the peasants, away from hearth and home, to go on with the lives that they lead. For some, misfortune and disaster pile up, but no migrant seems to think of packing his bags and returning home. Migrants don't like to give up. The city, no matter how cold and inhospitable it is at times, presents better prospects than the countryside.

For Chinese who want to do evil, the peasants are easy prey. A peasant who is in unknown territory is vulnerable. The local population picks them out easily—the result of a growing division between rich and poor.

When peasant simplicity still was the norm, all Chinese dressed in identical dark blue, black, or grey work clothes. But the years of shared poverty are past, and today's city dwellers wear tailor-made suits or nice clothing that is considered hip. Only the peasants have remained drab and threadbare.

That exterior has become decisive and determines how people are treated in Chinese society. Men with uncombed, uncut hair, heavy knit vests, worn jackets with the label still stitched on the sleeve, dark brown stains on their shirt collars, trousers held up by a rope or a strip of leather, very heavy long johns, transparent nylon kneesocks, and unwashed deep grooves in their skin are bound to be peasants, as every Chinese in the city will confirm.

Anyone who travels regularly by train, metro, or bus, especially on the busiest and cheapest routes in the country, will recognize the smell of unwashed bodies. That smell comes from the migrants, whose sweaty, dirty bodies lean against one another or lie on the floor, sleeping exhausted on their bundled blanket rolls.

The frightened black eyes in the weather-beaten peasant faces, or the amazed looks of the newcomers who are surprised at everything unknown, immediately betray their background. Migrant peasants can be recognized without fail. And in all their uncertainty, simplicity, and poverty, they are vulnerable victims for arrogant city dwellers, opportunistic managers, impatient officials, or corrupt police.

The twenty-seven unsuspecting peasants who arrived at the Dingzhou station in Hebei Province in the spring of 2000 must have looked like that. They had just finished a long and tiring journey and had come to this city in the northern Chinese province to look for work. Dingzhou lies in the midst of rich fields of grain, but what attracted the peasants from far and wide was the brick industry. The clay soil in the region not only is fertile but is also very suitable for firing bricks.

The prospect of steady work at one of the large ovens must have led the just-arrived peasants to accept the offer presented to them by a manager from one of these factories. The latter had no trouble picking the job-seeking men out of the traveling public. An agreement was soon made.

A year later the men made national news. The helpful manager turned out to be a recruiter who had put the peasants to work as slaves. No one knew about it, and none of the peasants were able to fight back. It wasn't until one of them managed to flee in May of 2001, more than a year after his arrival in Dingzhou, and the police raided the brick factory, that the affair came to light.

The men were easy prey for the brick factory bosses. As soon as they had been lured to one of the ovens in Sibiancun with the attractive promises of good pay, housing, and security, the atmosphere changed. The peasants were ordered to carry heavy clay and to stack fired bricks for twelve hours a day, but they were not paid. The peasants protested, but their arguments were ignored. According to the peasants, anyone who criticized or tried to escape got a good whipping. After several failed attempts, no one tried to flee anymore. Most had decided to get through their misery in the hope of getting out alive; they could not do anything else.

The fact that these twenty-seven men in Sibiancun were finally liberated is exceptional. Quite another lot has befallen many migrants, and they are still in similar situations. The Chinese media have regularly reported on slavery. Apparently this is not unusual in the kilns in the areas surrounding Shenzhen, of all places the city where migrant workers are accepted more than anywhere else in China.

In the 1990s, dozens of those brick ovens and stone quarries were closed in Guangdong Province, where Shenzhen is located. At one time the police in the province reported a "concentration camp," where workers were lured systematically and made to work. Eighty of them were liberated.

The government said that it had clamped down on the painful pre-revolutionary phenomenon of slavery. But in the spring of 2002, the *Dahe Ribao* from Henan reported on a raid at a coal mine with peasant slaves. The mine supervisors did not surrender without a struggle. Twenty-four heavily armed men were lying in wait for the police, and the gunfight that followed lasted all day.

Slavery is one of the peculiar excesses of burgeoning capitalism in the Chinese hinterland. But extorting labor is not unusual. Often local authorities seem to turn a blind eye in exchange for a part of the profit.

In this way migrant workers in the city are often forced to work because their pay is docked or withheld. Many Chinese employers initially refuse to pay wages regularly because they think that the newcomers should first prove that they can carry out their work obligations.

The manager of a large toy factory in Shenzhen expresses it as follows: "Migrants are cheap but unreliable employees. You never know what good they'll be. You train them, invest in them, and just when they function well and they start earning money for you, they quit—because the home front calls, because there is a better job, or simply because they no longer feel like it. You don't get to hear that from the employees themselves. They say nothing. They leave from one day to the next, and then you are suddenly without." For that reason, says the factory manager, more and more employers are prepared to take measures themselves. "They collect identity cards and pay only after three months or half a year. That's clever. If a worker leaves, you have at least saved on the pay."

At the end of 2003, the All-China Federation of Trade Unions calculated that because of these practices, Chinese companies owed migrant workers at least $11.5 billion. Moreover, this involved only discovered nonpayments for that year. Prime Minister Wen Jiabao spoke out against this practice and urged all companies, especially building contractors and restaurants, to pay overdue wages before the start of the Chinese New Year in 2004.

He did this by following the example of Zhengzhou, in Henan, where in 2002 a new rule went into effect that obliged all building contractors to pay their workers before the start of the New Year. If they neglected do this, then they could lose their building permits. It was an effective measure.

Chinese workers have practically no rights, but migrant workers are really unprotected. When the deadly pulmonary disease SARS broke out in the spring of 2003, the migrant workers in particular were the fall guys (except, of course, for the patients). Because it was feared that the illness, to which 348 people had succumbed in China, was being spread by the migrants, the government ordered them not to move around anymore. Newcomers were kept out of the city, and the peasants who were already in the city were "interned" in their workplaces.

But the panic was so great that, despite a prohibition that was in force, migrants were dismissed and banned everywhere. The Chinese Academy of Social Sciences calculated subsequently that during the months that the illness was abroad, at least 7 million migrant workers lost their jobs.

Migrant workers had a hard time protecting themselves at that time, and this is still true, despite government efforts to make changes. They are hampered by an obsolete Stalinist system that from their birth imposes limitations on them and deprives them of the right to reasonable and just treatment in Chinese society.

That system, which has condemned the peasants of China to their land for almost half a century and has made an honest and normal life in the city officially impossible for them, is called *hukouzhidu*, freely translated as "the system of family registration." Ideologically it is a completely noncommunist principle that establishes the division between city and countryside, a class difference between peasants and city dwellers—where the peasants are socially inferior to their fellow countrymen in the city—on the basis of birth.

But it is a principle that is part of China's long tradition of rank. The class system has existed for as long as China has had rulers. The irony of history is that the Communist rulers wanted to put an end to it. But that wish did not last long.

A popular explanation for the introduction of family registration is that it helped the supreme leader Mao Zedong in tracking down his "class enemies." The compulsory and detailed registration of the Chinese people gave the Communist leaders a convenient control apparatus for establishing all activities of the population and restricting them if necessary.

But there is more to this story. The restriction on the population's freedom of movement is above all what the registration system has become and how it has been implemented by the authorities to date. Its origin was different.

Right after the People's Republic was proclaimed in 1949, the Chinese leaders actually encouraged the process of urbanization. At that time the cities were still considered the engines of social and economic prosperity—a modernistic aspiration that did not seem irresponsible with a population of (only) 400 million Chinese. Between 20 million and 50 million peasants responded to that call and moved to the city. But with the famines at the end of the 1950s, resulting from the total failure of the Great Leap Forward, maintaining the social order was suddenly of political interest.

As everywhere, the peasants were self-supporting, but the growing cities had become more and more dependent on a government-controlled food network. After the Great Leap, food coupons were introduced so that no city dweller would starve in times of crisis.

But the collectivization of agriculture, which was introduced on a national level after 1956, also necessitated restricting the peasant class to the land. Party critics who had ideological objections to the violation of the socialist principle of equality—the status of farmers became equal once again to that of a serf—were mercilessly expelled from the party by Mao.

Mao needed the peasants. In the isolated and undeveloped China of the 1950s, the peasants were his most important capital. He praised them for their support of the Communist revolution, but at the same time he increased the gap between them and the rest of Chinese society by completely curbing the mobility of the peasant population.

This gap has only increased over the years and was at its worst during the mid-1970s. It was becoming an insoluble problem, comparable to the distinction between nobility and the people during the European Middle Ages, when birth determined an individual's opportunities in society.

It was not until 1979, after the death of Mao and the introduction of the first socialist market principles, that peasants were allowed to come to the city in small numbers. That "revolutionary" about-face did not come a moment too soon.

Through a politically motivated stimulation of population growth, the population in the countryside had increased explosively and threatened to create an unmanageable surplus of hidden unemployed persons. Moreover, in the city, which had become completely run-down during the years of upheaval and revolution, there was a great need for new workers who could give new muscle to the new political and economic programs from Beijing. This is how the work of peasants in the city came to be legalized by decree in 1982.

But the existing class distinction between peasants and city dwellers did not disappear. The system of family registration continued. The peasants were allowed to come and work in the city, but they still could not live there officially. For most of the migrant workers who came from far and wide, this situation was of course impossible. That is why the Chinese government tolerated their long stays. In this way the peasants got a firm foothold in the cities for the first time in twenty years.

The stream of peasants who found work in the cities grew steadily, and everyone was the better for it. But in the early 1990s, the mass migration started to take on unmanageable forms that became especially evident during the weeks around Chinese New Year, when all the migrants returned home to deposit their saved wages at the home front.

The numbers of travelers were staggering and still are. The Chinese news agency Xinhua reported in January 2006 that the Chinese had taken as many as 2 billion trips during the holidays. The news agency announced that 500 million Chinese, mostly migrant workers, had gone back home. Together they had taken 1.58 billion bus rides, 130 million train trips, and 7.5 million plane trips. The south Chinese city of Guangzhou handled 800,000 passengers daily. The numbers were preposterous, but one thing was clear: The number of migrants threatened to flood the cities.

There are still extensive discussions about the socioeconomic consequences of the migration and the continued existence of the system of family registration. In the meantime there has been experimentation at different governmental levels with adjusting or partially abolishing the system. In 2002, People's Congress Representative Chen Lini introduced a motion in which she advocated "freedom of migration" based on the international Covenant for Political Rights signed in 1998. It was a daring proposal, but one that was in keeping with reality. Two years later a bill was introduced in which the forty-five-year-old registration system was supposed to lapse. Registration would be permitted only for establishing one's identity. Various people pointed out that the system was old and out of date. For instance, it turned out that Shenzhen had 10 million registered inhabitants, of whom only 1.5 million were registered as "urban." Three million had a permanent residence permit, but more than 5 million people, some of whom had lived in the city for more than ten years, were officially still registered as "peasants." Wang Chunguang, associated with the Chinese Academy for Social Sciences, warned, "Many of [the migrants] have lived and worked in the city for more than twenty years. They no longer have any land or farming know-how. If the cities don't accept them, where can they go?" In reality, the distinction between the city and "the rest" is still huge in the minds of the authorities and the inhabitants of the city.

In the large cities the authorities apply a policy of determent. Migrant workers' lives are still not made easy, despite the economically vital role that they play in these cities. And the police force plays a big role by making sure that the peasants' papers can be checked at any time. In addition, the peasants are allowed to work and live only in very limited areas. They are in fact denied the right to education, medical care, and social care, despite new rules and laws that prohibit discrimination. Depending on the mood of the local authorities, peasants on the outskirts of the cities are rounded up without restraint, temporarily imprisoned, and sent home, without regard to the validity of their papers and the laws that actually forbid this practice.

The agencies that for many years dealt with punishing detained migrant workers were the so-called Centers for Detention and Repatriation. These were prisons where thousands of peasant workers who had been rounded up prior to national holidays or visits by dignitaries, or during political campaigns, were put up temporarily.

Until the summer of 2003, China had more than eight hundred of these centers. According to Chinese data, during the first six months of 2000, 180,000 migrant workers were rounded up in Beijing alone and locked up in the Center for Detention and Repatriation in Changping, just north of the capital.

In June of 2003 there was an official end to this arbitrary penal system when the twenty-year-old vagrancy law was abolished. This law, which was introduced in 1982 by the State Council (the cabinet) but was never ratified by the People's Congress (the parliament), stipulated that those without legal status in the city could be sent back without mercy to their village of origin. This illegal law was used for years by the police to exclude undesired peasants from the city.

But when in March of 2003 there was a big story in the news that the laws had been used against a jobless student, alarm bells started to ring in Beijing. What had happened? The police in the south Chinese city of Guangzhou had detained a twenty-seven-year-old graphic designer in the street at night. Because he had no identity papers with him, he was taken to the police bureau and locked up. According to the vagrancy law, this was permitted. But because the young man had resisted his treatment, he had by order of the police been beaten up by his fellow prisoners—causing his death.

The case leaked out and was picked up by several national newspapers; three young lawyers from Beijing considered it the right time to file a petition with the People's Congress. Their request was simple but daring: Implement the Chinese constitution and offer the migrant workers the protection to which they are actually entitled.

The reaction of the Chinese government was as unexpected as it was far-reaching: The vagrancy law was repealed and the Centers for Detention and Repatriation were closed. In addition, the Chinese government promised to study new rules concerning the rights of migrant workers.

Teng Biao, one of the petition's initiators, was euphoric. But he also expressed his doubts to the Chinese and foreign media. "We must make sure that the new rules don't contain exceptions that are just as bad as the old rules," he says. This was not an empty warning, for the police have retained the right to arrest as they see fit. In practice this means that the police can still condemn suspects to three years of forced labor without any trial. A careful discussion about the necessity and legality of this form of administrative detention was begun at the end of 2003.

In 2005 the Beijing city government took the lead by rescinding a ten-year-old rule that prohibited migrants from accepting certain jobs or living anywhere they wanted. Zhou Jidong, the director of the legal department of the administration of the capital, was matter-of-fact about that important step. "The [old] rules are in conflict with all principles of the market economy and are not workable in practice." Why had these rules existed for so long? "You can't eliminate the vestiges of the planned economy so easily," said Wang Yukai of the Chinese National School of Administration in a discussion with the Chinese news agency Xinhua. "There was simply no respect for the civil rights of fellow citizens."

But the decision was hardly made when there were meetings about other ways to limit the stream of migrants to the city. Representative Zhang Weiying, a member of the Communist Party People's Consultative Conference, had the nerve to propose closing the city gates once again. "The city is overburdened. Large, uncontrolled groups of migrants are streaming into the city without a stable income or a fixed place to live. That is a great threat for Beijing." There was a great stir among the other delegates, for it turned out that Zhang's words struck a sympathetic chord.

Despite new rules and intentions, the migrant workers are far from safe. For the time being, there is no end to the discriminating regulations. According to the State Development and Planning Commission, it is practically impossible to offer social security to the migrant peasants because they don't have a fixed place of residence. The commission pointed out, of course, that peasants can always fall back on their land, and that is better than nothing.

Migrant workers also find serious obstacles in the fact that they don't have any right to medical treatment. Local media report that in a city of migrants such as Shenzhen, forty-one people became handicapped daily in 2002 because of industrial accidents, and every four and a half days a worker died for that same reason. Ninety percent of the victims lost fingers, hands, or even whole arms. Most of these victims were migrant workers. Those who have lived to tell about it speak of a moment of inattention, lack of sleep, and the monotonous repetition of an action. In the Pearl River Delta alone, where most of the factories are located, thirty thousand people are injured each year. After an investigation in the summer of 2005, the Chinese State Administration for Work Safety found that in recent years in all of China, an average of fifteen thousand people were killed per year by industrial accidents.

Those who manage to survive always run the risk that they won't be treated for their injuries. Early in 2006 the *Heilongjiang Morning Post* published a big story about a worker, Wang Jianmin, who had bled to death in a hospital in Beijing because the Emergency Care ward had refused him admission for financial reasons. The victim, a migrant worker, had no cash on him.

Few factories feel responsible for their workers. In the contracts, if there are any, nothing is set down about responsibility for medical care. And because the employees are not registered in the city, most factory managers feel under no obligation at all. An average peasant employee can feel lucky if his employer takes on the medical costs of an accident, but most victims never receive compensation.

The local authorities go along with this practice and support the companies. In Shenzhen, only residents who are registered there have the right to accident insurance, not migrant workers. The authorities believe that benefits and medical treatment cannot be provided if a worker does not have a fixed place of residence in the city. The reasoning is that the responsibility for these people lies with the villages where the workers are registered.

Zhou Litai, a lawyer from Shenzhen, thinks that is "ridiculous." He is one of the few who are concerned about migrant workers injured in industrial accidents. "The local authorities force the migrant workers to return to their villages for medical treatment. But in that way they run the chance of losing their job in exchange for their health. The local authorities refuse to take responsibility for the migrants, who, after all, are an important stimulus for their economy," says Zhou. And that, he feels, is frankly discriminating.

For that reason Zhou has over the years taken care of many injured migrant workers. He takes a stand against companies that were negligent or against the Bureau of Social Security. In addition he houses the peasant victims if need be. On average, thirty of them stay in his house at any one time.

Strikingly, Zhou has had unparalleled success. Most of the hundreds of charges that he has lodged in Shenzhen since 1997 have been upheld. In 90 percent of the cases, his charges against the factories in question have achieved results—not that this has made him rich. The reality is that as soon as the peasants are helped and compensated, they leave with all their money, without thanking Zhou for his help or repaying him.

Zhou's actions are not liked at all by the Chinese government, since it is afraid of a storm of complaints that might scare off factory managers and make them decide to establish their companies elsewhere. In Shenzhen several factory managers, especially Taiwanese ones, have already threatened to leave the city if the city government does not stop people like Zhou Litai. The city government supports these employers with the argument that "industrial accidents are after all the consequence of economic progress." This point of view is shared by the Chinese Ministry of Labor.

Yet several cities in China—among them Chengdu, Shanghai, and Guangdong—proposed in 2002 making it mandatory for companies to take out accident insurance for all their employees. But the central government is not prepared to support even this plan. According to the State Development and Planning Commission, required insurance might prevent companies from hiring migrants and could slow down the process of urbanization—a process that the commission wants to accelerate. Urbanization goes before workers' rights.

This same state commission is also responsible for a decision that will most certainly help the migrants in the long run. It decided in August 2001 to abolish in stages the system of family registration.

One of the main reasons for that important decision was that the stream of migrants to the city had become so massive that it could no longer be held back. Every year between 5 and 6 million peasants would join the army of 150 million surplus peasants, according to the state commission's calculations. And in five years the large cities would expand by at least 46 million.

The cabinet decision was not supported enthusiastically everywhere. Even within the government, opinions were divided. After public transportation had been disrupted once again for a month during the Chinese New Year in 2002, Bao Suixian, the former deputy director of the Ministry of Public Security, said that abolishing the system of family registration would be completely out of the question. According to Bao, the system was an indispensable link in preserving public safety.

The last word has not been spoken on this subject. The fact is that in numerous places in China, a careful dismantling of this apartheid system has begun. Some large cities had already started this process in the past. In these places migrant workers received a residence permit for the city when they had demonstrated that they were successful. The requirements differed from city to city, but most of the time the peasants in question had to have a steady income for some time, pay taxes, have bought a house, or have a certain number

Inner courtyard of a cannery, Shenzhen (Yang Yankang)

of employees from the city working for them. These seem nearly impossible requirements for the masses, and the number of new applications remained manageably low—precisely the way many of these experimenting city governments had intended.

In the south Chinese province of Guangdong, the province with the most migrant workers in China, the system was for the first time overhauled on a large scale in December 2001. The admission quotas that were still in effect there were permanently abolished, and now every city, except for Guangzhou and Shenzhen, is allowed to decide who may and who may not settle there. The admission system in Guangzhou and Shenzhen has become much stricter. In 2002, the city government in those cities established a ban on attracting new migrant workers.

A test project in fifteen districts in Hunan Province, where migrants were allowed to settle freely, was so successful that companies there no longer wanted a different policy. The gap between poor and rich decreased, and according to the local media, the factory managers declared that it was a relief in comparison with the strict rules of the past. It had suddenly become administratively very simple to hire peasants, and more and more "good" companies were ready to employ migrants. Peasants who satisfied the "criteria" received a residency permit for the city, the right to work, medical care, and a pension. How exactly these benefits were being financed was not mentioned.

In Shijiazhuang, the capital of Hebei, abolishing the family registration system created a surprise. The city government was very keen to bring in migrants to stimulate the local economy. But very few peasants seized that chance. Those who did were already registered in the city. The city government didn't understand this result at all and carried out an inquiry. The conclusion was alarming: After all these years of discrimination, most migrant workers preferred to do without these city rights. They had learned to survive the hard way and harbored a deep distrust of the city government. Most peasants preferred to remain illegal.

Wu Guihua, mother of Bai Chuiying

CUTTING HAIR WITHOUT SEX

Wu Guihua, Mother of Chuiying

"Sometimes I'm jealous of Chuiying," says forty-seven-year-old Wu Guihua. "When I was twenty-two, I was already married. Chuiying has so
many more opportunities."

Since her children, two daughters and a son, have left home, Wu has been on her own. Her husband was killed five years ago when a wall next to their house where he was working collapsed and completely buried him. "I thought that the world had stopped existing," she says about the tragic accident.

She is proud of Chuiying. "According to tradition it's the sons who go and study, but my daughters are much smarter." Her son did not finish junior high school and now works in a garage in a small provincial town far away from the village. He left when he was only fourteen years old. "I tried to talk to him, but he doesn't listen anyway."

When Chuiying, the apple of her eye, left, she cried for a whole week. But Wu could understand her decision. "I was so worried. I dared to let her go only because her classmate Li Yanhong was already in Beijing."

Meanwhile, Wu's distress has turned into pride. "She makes use of her opportunities," says Wu. In her own youth Beijing was still inaccessible. "We heard about it from the village committee's loudspeakers." There was daily news from Beijing about the revolution, production numbers, and party ideology. Except for love, there was little to do in the village, according to Wu. "There was meeting and studying, meeting and studying, meeting and studying. That was during the Cultural Revolution. If you wanted to go to Beijing during that time, you needed three documents to get permission. No, I'm glad that my daughter has seized the new opportunities of this existence with both hands."

Bai Chuiying, Hairdresser, Changping

"Beijing is very different from what I had imagined," says twenty-two-year-old Chuiying. She was seventeen when she left Shangdouyin. Encouraged by her former classmate Yanhong, she joined her girlfriend, who was already in Beijing and starting training to be a hairdresser. After one and a half years she finished and went to look for work. That was a horrible experience.

Bai Chuiying

   "When you live in the countryside you don't know any better than that the city is the way it is depicted on television and in the newspapers. Beautiful and modern." But Chuiying now knows that the reality is different.

   "There was no employer who wanted me to do what I was trained for: cut hair." Her first job lasted exactly four days. "I had told the owner what I could do and wanted to do. He agreed to that." But she hadn't been working for five minutes on the haircut of a male client when he asked for "more"— a euphemism for sex. "I answered that I was no good at 'more' and that he'd better ask one of the other girls. He was not satisfied with that."

Instead of supporting her, her boss got angry. Contrary to their agreement, he said to Chuiying that she had to satisfy her clients' wishes. Chuiying refused. " 'You can earn more money this way,' he said. But I didn't want to. Then he fired me on the spot. In those four days I had earned $6."

Her female colleagues did not understand her attitude. "They do what the clients ask of them, as long as they earn money," says Chuiying. "They earn $600 a month, four times as much as with just cutting hair. For many girls the temptation is irresistible."

Many hairdresser's jobs followed; several times she quit. She is again looking for work, just hairdresser's work, nothing more. Her potential bosses demand that she hand over her identity card as security. "That's very risky. Before you know it, you're stuck."

Chuiying realizes that many peasant parents worry about their daughters precisely because of such stories. But, says Chuiying, her mother knows that her daughter knows her limits.

In the long run, Chuiying would like nothing better than to return to her native village, but only when she has earned back the investment of her training and has enough money to open her own hairdressing salon in Shangdouyin. "I want to be a role model for other peasant girls," she says thoughtfully. "I want them to see that peasants have opportunities, too, and can profit from the city."

She is sixteen, perhaps seventeen. A.V. doesn't know exactly. "But I'm old enough to take care of myself," she says. She does everything for Xiaowu, her friend. She is his most important source of income. Because A.V. is constantly ill, becomes pregnant, and then gets an abortion, she feels weak. That is why she let a doctor apply a drip/infusion "with a tonic." She prefers to recover at home. "It's cheaper."

Purchased Innocence

Offering Their Bodies

(Hainan, Haikou, Zhongguocheng)

No one knows how far the dolled-up peasant daughters will go. The women, *xiaojie* or "ladies," like to keep their clients in suspense. They look brazenly at the men, play up their awkwardness, freshen the men's drinks generously, and voluptuously place a leg over that of their partner for the evening. There is loud talking and vulgar laughter. The men pull at them, and the women let them carry on. It isn't much more. Far past midnight the men head drunkenly to their hotel. The women remain behind, exhausted but a little richer.

Because Zhongguocheng, or "Chinatown," in the port city of Hainan is a public building, the managers of the pleasure complex say that everything that happens there is innocent and that the women who work there are free to show importunate clients the door. The women themselves echo that. But who believes it?

One of the *mamis*, female pimps, talks freely. She feels that she has nothing to lose. She knows that the power of the *jitou*, or "chickenheads" (pimps), reaches into the villages where the peasant daughters come from. That is why, according to her, there are no limits at all in Zhongguocheng. The "chicken-heads" put pressure on their flock and threaten to inform the girls' parents about the depraved secret lives of their daughters, who have lost their innocence for good. For most girls the very threat of losing face in front of their parents is sufficiently intimidating.

Under the flickering light of a yellow neon lamp, in a dark corner of a nightclub on the third floor of Zhongguocheng, sits a girl who doesn't feel at ease. She bites her lip, wobbles with one leg on the immense heel of her platform shoe, and looks around nervously. Her eyes are hidden behind a dyed red lock of hair. "Yang Quan," she whispers her name. But is that really her name? *Jiaming, jiaxing, jia dizhi—pianchi, pianhe, pian ganqing*, a bankrupt nightclub owner had told me beforehand. "Fake first name, fake last name, fake address—sham eating, sham drinking, and sham feelings. Nothing that they say or do is genuine." Those are supposed to be the protection mechanisms learned by all country girls in the nightclubs of Hainan.

But "Yang Quan" doesn't look like an accomplished con artist. She has been in Haikou for exactly six days, and it's her first time ever in a big city. She says that she's eighteen. She has not yet mastered the profession of purchased love and the playacting that is part of it. She is a bundle of nerves, and her smile is unconvincing. In her pink-flowered dress and white platform shoes that are still shiny and new, she doesn't look like a country girl. But her genuine innocence reveals that she has only very recently become acquainted with the world of urban deceit. Her first days in Zhongguocheng were no success.

"I refused twice," she says softly. It's called *tuitai*, or "giving up the table." The opposite, necking with a client on a sagging small sofa in one of the stuffy alcoves of the nightclub, is called *zuotai*, "working the table." "When you ditch a client, you get into trouble with your *mami*." But Yang Quan didn't care.

"He behaved discourteously," she says about one of her first customers. "He wanted to touch me everywhere, and I didn't want that." The way she says it sounds childish, but she looks betrayed. Does Yang Quan really not know that that's the only thing for which men who visit Zhongguocheng have come?

A.V. has steady customers. They always come back to her. Once in a while, one of them befriends her, like this man—but not until after sharing her bed.

This is what Haikou, and actually all of Hainan, is known for. The subtropical island in the southern part of the country is a place of unrestrained pleasure, where men—corrupt executives, according to the people—openly take pleasure with the generous supply of unspoiled female beauty. That beauty, or what passes for it, has steadily found its way from the peasant hinterland to Haikou.

The numerous sex clubs—nowhere in China are there as many, and nowhere are they as easy to find, as in Haikou—date from the heyday of the real estate explosion. That was in the early 1990s, when many a local government came to invest in apartments and buildings that, it turned out later, would never be sold. Busloads of officials came to inspect the building of their very expensive projects, at the expense of the state and attracted by the nice

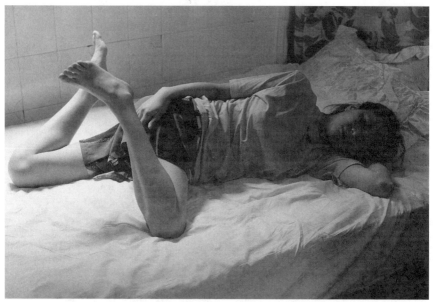

When Xiao Li was seven years old, her mother died. Her father left his children behind by themselves. Her grandparents took care of her. In order to relieve them of that burden, Xiao Li decided to go to work at a young age. She started at a shipping company along the Yangtze. There she met Xiao Ou. He was her great love. She put together all her savings with his and bought a tuk-tuk (or auto rickshaw). But not long after that, three men robbed Xiao Ou of his tuk-tuk and murdered him. Destitute and desperate, Xiao Li left for Hainan in 1993.

climate and the nightclubs that popped up faster than their own projects. The places of innocent entertainment turned out to offer more than just drink, song, and conviviality—as long as you paid.

At that time as many as three thousand women—every one of them a young girl from a disadvantaged province—worked in Zhongguocheng, a complex that looks like a run-down five-floor warehouse. "It was black with people here," declares Li Xiaomei, a fifty-year-old woman who wears her gray hair wound around her head like cotton candy. She is a dance teacher and has taught dancing to numerous peasant girls who went to work in Zhongguocheng. It has left her with a mission: She is totally convinced that when she teaches "her" girls to dance, it is possible for them to escape prostitution. "Anyone who starts as a lady companion ends as a prostitute and probably ends up on drugs," she says, convinced. "By teaching these women a trade, I offer them an alternative. But they do have to do their bit."

Xiaomei, a perky lady who shows off her "artistic" personality, knows Zhongguocheng and the other nightclubs of Haikou like the back of her hand. Money must have flowed here like water. "I encountered everyone who was anyone here," she says. "I couldn't believe what I saw! Policemen, provincial leaders, party bureaucrats, directors of government enterprises—they all came!"

Now only the echo of these wild days reverberates in the cavernous spaces of Zhongguocheng. With the collapse of the real estate market several years later, the customers disappeared, too. The steady trek of peasant girls to Hainan also decreased, and what remains is a desolate atmosphere. "Only the most innocent, the neediest, and the poorest still visit Haikou," says Xiaomei about the dozens of girls who hang around there.

Yang Quan says that she knew nothing about any of this. Before she went to Hainan, she worked as a chambermaid in a hotel in a suburb of Tongren, in Guizhou Province. "It was a fine job, but it didn't pay much," she says. When a colleague mentioned similar but better-paid work in Haikou, she and a girlfriend decided to go for it. "That colleague said that he had a sister in Haikou who could get us work. I liked that boy; it sounded reliable." The pay would be 100 yuan more than the 300 yuan that Yang Quan had earned until then. Though the difference was only $13, for Yang Quan this was plenty attractive.

Once in Haikou, after a trip that had cost her all her savings, Yang Quan learned that her colleague's sister was a *mami*. Yang Quan and her friend, who by then were broke, were immediately sent to Zhongguocheng and brought in to "amuse" customers.

Yang Quan doesn't want to say what she thinks of this, but the fact that every morning she gets up again at seven o'clock after working all night until half past one speaks volumes. "I don't know what to say to these men." She giggles nervously. She has never had a boyfriend and says she doesn't know how to please men. Most of the time she looks incredulously at her new colleagues in the adjoining alcoves, who find it easy. They keep the men satisfied, get hefty tips, and sometimes know how to prevent too many intimacies.

Yang Quan's *mami*, the sister of her former colleague from Tongren, watches her newest acquisition suspiciously from the nightclub entrance. The peasant girl's reluctant attitude doesn't please her at all. Clientele is in short supply, and she can't afford dissatisfied customers since the nightclub on the third floor of Zhongguocheng—the higher the floor, the lower the "quality" of the women—is practically empty.

On a stage stands a girl with braids wearing a shiny space suit who is singing sentimental Chinese songs. Her microphone is much too loud and her voice resounds through the low-ceilinged space. Behind a long bar, dozens of dolled-up peasant daughters sit and wait indifferently for customers who don't come. Their hair is combed into peaks, their faces are dusted with glitter, their lips are painted red, their eyebrows are accentuated in black, and on their bodies are creations that are particularly conspicuous because of their metallic colors and futuristic fashion.

It is a dingy place, and the whole atmosphere seems dirty. But fortunately it's so dark that the guests miss most of it, even if they had an eye for it. There is just enough light to find the way, but not enough to be able to see what is happening on the sofas.

There is dancing, mostly in the dark, there is singing, and there is a lottery. A quizmaster comments on everything and plays games. A group of dancing and singing girls, perhaps pupils of Li Xiaomei, conclude the show.

It has not been an edifying evening. The show was bad. But no one cares about that. The entertainment is secondary to what happens in the alcoves.

Yang Quan settles up. From every 200 yuan that she pockets per customer,

20 yuan go to her *mami*. But companion girls are also expected to succeed in wheedling good-size tips from their clients in addition to the arranged price. That tip is for their *mami* as well. And she is not satisfied with less than 100 yuan. "If I don't manage that, she gets angry," says Yang Quan about her *mami*. She has never managed it. She is unhappy about this and longs for home. But she is stuck. Yang Quan doesn't have a red cent. That's why she stays in Zhongguocheng—just until she has saved the $54 for the trip back to Tongren.

EVIL STEPMOTHERS

Mamis are like evil stepmothers. They look after their "children" with feigned love, and assist them in work and deed and with money, but they change into rigid mistresses who chastise their girls harshly when the dependent peasant daughters don't keep their word. In the end most of the girls accept this voluntary dependency, for without *mami* there are no customers, and without customers there is no income.

Wang Hong is a tall, forty-five-year-old woman. She is originally from Jilin Province but her workplace is in the busiest nightclub in the city. It is located in a narrow alley near the old center of Haikou and is an establishment that caters exclusively to the needs of the local public. There can be such a rush that the peasant girls are lined up and ready in two rows at both sides of the narrow stairs that give access to the complex. Most customers are waylaid from all sides and then enter through a plastic swinging door with a woman they fancy.

Wang Hong introduces herself with two skinny girls in her wake. There is no doubt at all—her directness and her clothing (a black suit with a matching black leather purse, cream-colored shoes, calf-length nylon socks—the hallmark of a peasant woman who wants to be citified) make immediately clear who she is. This is a *mami* of stature.

She looks at me questioningly and defiantly—what could my desires possibly be? I answer that I am looking for a woman from Sichuan. "I'm from Sichuan," she says, teasing. I get no chance to react. She pushes me into the dark room, through a crowd of women, down a staircase, through a labyrinth of narrow passages, and into a room. Then she disappears suddenly. In the small room there are some easy chairs, a karaoke television that is on, and two microphones at the ready. From behind the wall there are sounds of desultory and off-key singing, men's voices and women's voices, several at the same time—all of them sounding silly and uncontrolled.

Then the door swings open. It's Wang Hong with a serious-looking girl at her side. Through the doorway, curious and white-powdered faces look inside. The girl that Wang Hong has brought along is very young. And just like Yang Quan in Zhongguocheng, this girl moves uncomfortably in the rather un-subtle creation that she is wearing—white pants that are much too tight and a flowered blouse with holes. The girl, who says that her name is Luo Xiaofeng, keeps sticking her tongue through her teeth in embarrassment.

But then the door opens wide once again. A woman with long straight hair starts scolding Xiaofeng in dialect and gestures for her to come along. She has the same serious look as the young girl. Xiaofeng obeys willingly and leaves without saying a word.

"Her aunt," Wang Hong apologizes. The woman in question was Xiaofeng's most important contact in Hainan's underworld, and she was clearly afraid of her inexperienced and clumsy niece's strange customer.

Mami Wang Hong sighs deeply and sits down on the sofa. "I have no influence on the women I manage," she complains after it has become clear to her that I am looking for something besides sex. "I get 20 yuan broker's costs," but if her girls are called away by their pimps or recruiters, then she gets nothing. She leans forward, wants to leave again to look for another girl, but sinks back onto the sofa.

"*Mamis* don't have it easy," she says. "You have to know what your customer wants. I listen to his wishes. If he asks for a girl who can sing beautifully, then I get him that. This is a difficult year. There are a lot of girls but no customers. I spend a lot but I earn too little."

Wang Hong acts as a go-between for twenty girls, but she is uncertain that these peasant girls will be loyal to her. "They have no obligations," she says, "but I do." The nightclub has eight *mamis*, each of whom has to hand over 400 yuan in order to be allowed to operate there.

"I put almost all of my money in my son's schooling." Her eyes stray to her black purse from which, after rummaging impatiently, she produces a crumpled photo of a boy with a crew cut and a roguish face. "I'm the only one he can fall back on."

Wang is divorced. Until 1997 she worked at a local tea factory. But when the factory was closed by the province, she lost her job. "I worked there from 1976 and then was out on the street from one day to the next," she says. She is still indignant about it.

She left the 12,000 yuan ($1,450) that she received upon her forced dismissal untouched for months. "I felt paralyzed—I didn't know what to do." In the end she used the money to open a teahouse for retirees. "I became self-employed."

At first the place ran well, but Wang was her own best customer at the teahouse and gambled away practically all her money during the daily mah-jongg games with her elderly customers. "I was open from one until six and asked 1 yuan per cup of tea. After eight, new customers came and played mah-jongg until deep into the night. I joined in but lost everything I had earned that day." Wang fell into her own trap and went bankrupt.

An unmarried woman told her about Haikou. "She saw that I was down and out and at my wit's end. She said that she could arrange a job of 1,000 yuan [$130] a month. I had to provide for a child," she says apologetically. Wang Hong did not hesitate and decided to accept the offer. "That neighbor had it made, I could tell from her clothes. I was impressed."

She did not tell her elderly mother, who was taking care of her son, anything except that she had found work. "In my misery I feel connected to her," she says about her mother. "She's also had it rough. My parents divorced in 1968 because my father was condemned as *huaifenzi* [bad element] during the Cultural Revolution." Wang Hong was raised by her mother, who remarried, but her new husband died after a few years. In 1978, two years after the end of the Cultural Revolution, Wang's mother visited her first husband, but he had become so embittered about what had happened that he wanted no more contact with his former family.

"As a single mother I wanted to give my child a better future than what my mother was able to give me," she concludes.

When Wang Hong arrived in Haikou, she was very insecure. "I was forty, but I felt just like these very young newcomers. That's why I always stood in the back of the crowd; I felt out of place among all that young fry." She says that she earned very little. Eventually she met an older man who felt attracted to slightly older Wang. "He asked me if I could dance. I said, 'Only the cha-cha-cha.' And that was true. He laughed and immediately noticed that I wasn't an ordinary woman," she says, not without pride. "We danced all evening. At the end he gave me 50 yuan [$6.20]. I was so happy! I'd never earned that much in one evening."

Later they met more often. "He took care of me, gave me money; I could save again. He was good to me. He accepted me as I was. I felt taken seriously," she says dreamily. But one day he disappeared from her life. "That's how it is in this work," she says knowingly.

Wang suspects that the wife of her steady customer had got wind of his meetings with her. "I never again had contact with him," she says, disappointed. She means it. "I never asked what he did exactly; I didn't dare to, and it isn't done." But she is sure that he was a bigwig in the Hainan provincial government.

"He didn't care for young girls," she concludes. "Young girls are very problematic." But it's the young girls that most men go for. "The older the men, the greater the need for young flesh."

Country girls who dream of wealth are easily influenced by fellow villagers who return home one fine day in a fur coat and with a fat wallet. This is how most girls have found their way to Hainan.

BEING POOR IS WORSE

Wang Hong's family does not know about the double life that she leads. Once a month she sends them money, and that's it—500 yuan ($60) to provide for her son and 200 yuan for her mother.

"My son visited last year," Wang Hong relates. "He wanted to see where his mother works. I took him to an amusement park, we went out to dinner, and he saw the ocean." But they didn't go to the area of the nightclubs. "Of course I told him nothing. It was a difficult week, but he had a good time."

She starts to cry. "I'm not here for the fun of it. I'm doing all of it for him and am stopping as soon as he has graduated." Her son's schooling—he's at the agricultural college in Chengdu—costs her a great deal of money and great personal sacrifices. She recounts what she has suffered. "Once I was beaten and didn't dare to go on the street for a month," she says. "That often happens here." Yet things are much better for her as a *mami* than for most of the peasant girls who end up here.

"Most of the girls are trapped. Their pimps, the 'chickenheads,' operate from their own villages. The parents of these girls know most of these men and have no idea at all that they are dealing with real criminals." That's why they are confident that their daughters are in good hands. "These boys promise to send them 500 yuan or more. And the girls suspect nothing. They don't know what's awaiting them. They think that it will be all right with a recommendation from a villager or a more or less known acquaintance. But once in Hainan, they find out what their new work actually entails and that they have to hand over the greater part of their earnings to the 'chickenheads' or to their *mamis*. That's why it takes most of them a long time before they are able to leave here."

When the peasant girls return to their villages after several years, they share their painful past with no one because they are scared of the humiliation and the threats of the men from the village or the district who snared them.

Wang Hong knows that the young male peasants who work as pimps are especially on the lookout for virgins. "Customers pay big money for virgins— between 3,000 and 10,000 yuan [$1,250] for a night." Of course most of that money disappears into the pockets of the pimps.

Wang shakes her head and wipes away her tears. She detests the industry that she is part of, but she doesn't feel she is an accomplice in her role as *mami*. "There are two sides to it," she says. "Of course I sympathize with them and would like these girls, who sometimes are as old as my son, to be able to do other work. On the other side, I see that for most of us this suffering is of short duration and that the money you earn offers opportunities that you can never get after a life of physical labor on the land. "*Xiaopin, bu xiaochang*," says Wang

Hong; "rather a whore than poor. People look down on poverty. Poverty is humiliating. I can live with the shame of an indecent past."

SALUTING BLACK CARS

Wang Guan, Father of Wang Sujun

Ask fifty-one-year-old Wang Guan about the capital and he'll grab his ears. He was there once but did not care for it at all. "It's quieter here," he says. The prosperity has made no impression on him, yet he can understand Wang Sujun. "There is nothing to do for him here. The two of us can cultivate the land that we have," he says. His wife stands silently next to him. There is a long silence. The Wangs are people of few words.

Wang Guan and his wife, the parents of Wang Sujun

In the house hang posters and an old calendar with photos of young Chinese couples holding a bouquet and happily looking into the empty room. Nothing gives the impression that the Wangs have a son who works in the city. He sends them no money and visits them only once a year. It doesn't bother Wang Guan; more than that, he has never even thought about it. "If he ever becomes rich," he says, "then we'll see." He is resigned to the thought that Sujun is a "good boy who doesn't create problems." Then Wang Guan gets up, picks up a shovel, and leaves. His wife sweeps the sandy floor. There has been enough talking.

Wang Sujun

Wang Sujun, Guard, Beijing

Four hours on, eight hours off. There is not much job pressure for nine-teen-year-old Wang Sujun, but the work that he has is "boring." Sujun earns his money ($70 per month) by standing silently at attention. He "de-fends" the entrance of a district office in Beijing. He checks the papers of the employees of the unit, whether he knows them or not, for that is his task. And he jumps to attention for armored black cars without knowing who is inside. Sujun knows that those are party executives and that you jump aside for them.

"I don't have to do much more," says Sujun. The rest of his hours he stands at attention, studies the passersby in the narrow street, or dreams about the future. That future will take place in Beijing as far as he's concerned—his own garage and repairing cars is his dream. His job as guard is just the start of what is supposed to become a thriving career. This is just for the time being—to get a toehold in the big city, for it isn't all that easy.

"I've been disappointed here in Beijing," says Sujun. "The people from the city hear immediately whether you're one of them or not. They have no respect for people from the provinces." Sujun knows that peasants among themselves are not like that. "Peasant labor is no fun, but I don't look down on it. Without peasants, China is utterly lost," he says seriously. "After all, we take care that there is enough to eat. And you can't find a city dweller who is willing to stand for hours in front of such a gate."

Sujun would not want to go back to Shangdouyin for anything. "That would mean that I failed." Anyone who leaves the countryside does so in order never to return. His parents are resigned to that. Because "whatever happens, in the city you learn more than in the country."

任

The Cost of Rain

Corruption
(Jiangxi, Lanfang, Dongtougan)

Dongtougan village held its collective breath when a column of police cars came rumbling over the sandy path. The trees were bare, and on the clear winter day the flashing lights and dust clouds could be seen from a distance as they approached. When the cars reached the village, instead of uniformed policemen, a group of men in plain clothes with metal clubs in their hands got out of the car.

Resolutely they headed straight for the stone house with the white façade, at the top of a hill in the center of the village. That house belonged to Liang Jianping, a thirty-six-year-old peasant who had dared to complain about the high taxes that he and his fellow villagers had to cough up yearly.

Liang, who had not been warned, was taking a pee in his backyard. But when he realized that the sinister party was looking for him, he raced down the hill and made a run for it.

The drafty porch of Liang's house is crowded when he tells his story. In the meantime, two weeks have passed. The villagers squat down, grab stools, and lean against one another. Liang has a lot of supporters in Dongtougan. The village head puts his arms around Liang's and my shoulders in a brotherly way.

The peasants admire their skinny fellow villager. "They can come back any minute, but that doesn't stop me," says Liang brazenly. He is a man who stands up for himself and his fellow villagers. "If you come back here in five years, we'll all be in the slammer," he says. His friends laugh. "Yes, or a peasant revolt will have pushed the corrupt bureaucrats from their pedestal!"

The peasants in the entryway are excited. For the first time in their lives they have revolted against the established order. Nowhere else has this anger spread as much as here. The peasants in this district in the south Chinese agricultural province of Jiangxi have been paying more in taxes than they earn, and therefore all of them have large debts. The peasants say that their incomes have been going entirely to the arbitrary levies imposed on them by the local authority of Lanfang, which covers Dongtougan. And the officials confiscate in kind whatever the peasants can't pay. One peasant has had to give up a television set and furniture, another one his plows and his ox. But thanks to Liang's alertness, the peasants have for the first time become aware of their rights. Since then they have also let their presence be known.

The immediate cause for the peasant revolt was the publication of a small book written by a diligent journalist of a provincial magazine about agricultural affairs; in it all the officially permitted agricultural levies were listed. Liang noticed the book, *A Manual for Reduction of the Peasants' Taxes*, in a bookstore in the provincial capital. He immediately bought 140 copies and distributed them among the villagers.

It came as a bombshell. The peasants sat together for evenings on end and spelled it out page after page for the one or two individuals who had not yet received or understood it. What these peasants of Dongtougan had suspected for a long time was confirmed in black and white on these pages: Most of the levies that the Lanfang authorities came to collect with ever-increasing regularity were not allowed!

Urged on by the angry villagers, Liang, who had taken the lead several times in the past, left for Lanfang red-faced and with the book in his hand. *With this Imperial Sword in Their Hands, Our Peasant Friends Will Feel More Certain* was the subtitle of the handbook. As a matter of fact, Liang had never felt so strong. He went in person to get justice. The book was his proof. He would not let them mock him; he would pull out the small volume as his trump card.

At least Liang knew for sure that he had wrongfully been made to pay through the nose for years, that the slaughtering tax should be calculated per family and not per family member, that the chopping tax for cutting down a tree did not even exist, that a tax in the form of forced labor was forbidden, and levies for building a road or installing electrical cables in Jiangxi were not permitted.

The officials of Jiangxi were scared out of their wits. They looked at one another in disbelief, became angry, then wanted to study the text, and subsequently panicked. "You should know that we're under pressure, too," they informed Liang nervously. "We have to feed many mouths; we can't do otherwise." More excuses followed. But then the truth came out. Would Liang perhaps hand in the books in exchange for a good job as supervisor in the Bureau of Road Construction?—an offer that Liang turned down flatly. Justice was what he wanted. It infuriated the officials.

The provincial government was consulted. It turned out that Liang was not the only peasant in Jiangxi who had managed to get his hands on the book that opened his eyes. Everywhere in the province farmers summoned up their courage to openly announce their dissatisfaction. An alarmed government in the provincial capital, Nanchang, imposed restraints on the sale of the manual in all of Jiangxi. Local officials went door-to-door to confiscate all the books that were already in circulation. And Gui Xiaoqi, the official who had written the book, was fired and was unavailable for further comment.

In Jiangxi they were sick and tired of assertive peasants. At the end of August 2000, at least ten thousand peasants in Fengcheng, an adjoining district, had taken to the streets to protest unreasonable levies and corrupt tax officials. In four district centers the farmers, wild with anger, broke the windows of government buildings and plundered the homes of party members who were suspected of corruption. "This is not a political demonstration. We're trying to survive," said the peasants. But the authorities were unrelenting. Paramilitary troops were called in hurriedly and needed six days to restore order. Three peasants were killed, and more than forty others—agitators, according to the police—were arrested and imprisoned.

The unrest in Jiangxi was so extensive that it attracted the attention of the central authorities in Beijing. A special investigative team was sent to Fengcheng, and China's most important television station, China Central Television, for a short time was granted the freedom to report about the defense of peasant Liang and his comrades and the open refusal of the provincial government to comply with the national rules pertaining to the taxation of peasants.

In the program *The Economy—One Half Hour*, which presents unusually direct investigative journalism from China itself, a party member from Lanfang was convinced that certain levies were unacceptable. "But they expect us to have more income every year than in the year before." The official wanted to know how the journalist thought that they could meet that requirement from the central government. After all, didn't everyone know that the economy in the Chinese countryside was stagnating? "We are threatened with dismissal if no money is delivered, but we can't work miracles." When the reporter asked whether the official felt that he had the right to keep the peasants in ignorance by not informing them of the rules that were drawn up by the central authority, he ignored the question.

When the makers of *The Economy—One Half Hour* planned a follow-up broadcast, they heard from the powers that be that it could not be presented. The reason: The taxation question caused too much unrest among the peasants throughout the country and could possibly explode. Obviously the political leaders of the country were of two minds. They were willing to tackle the tax burden problem and even saw the necessity of doing it, but not if it would be at the expense of their control over the hinterland.

These worries were appropriate. In Beijing there is great alarm about the enormous and unstable hinterland. *Research About the Discrepancies Among the People in the New Circumstances*, a report from 2001 ordered by the party leadership, stated that corruption was the "fuse" in the conflict with the peasants and that income inequality in the country had reached "red alert." In 2005, twenty-four thousand officials were sued because of corruption—by no means sufficient, according to the Ministry of Justice, but at least it was something.

The *People's Daily* wrote that "only through stability in the countryside can stability in the country" be guaranteed. "Commotions create great unrest," Zhou Yongkang, the minister of public security, worried in 2005. "The numbers are increasing and threaten to become unmanageable."

The fact that the agricultural province Jiangxi of all places was in the news as a place of insolvent and corrupt officials was particularly painful for the party. For it was seventy years ago in Jiangxi that the Communist Party had one of their largest and strongest bases, and the support of the peasants had been the foundation of the Communist victory. If it was anywhere that the peasants had earned the special attention of the party, it was there.

Not a trace of the former revolutionary glory was to be found in Jiangxi. After many decades of independence and neglect, the party officials had become notoriously corrupt. Even the provincial government admitted this. In 2000 the party executive committee reported that in the past two years it had ejected as many as seventy-seven hundred members from the party for ideological reasons. At the end of the 1990s, the deputy governor of the province, Hu Changqing, was caught embezzling tax money. The central authorities decided to make an example of him and condemned him to death.

SALT CRYSTALS (Shaanxi, Zizhou)

Was it by chance that peasant discontent was again brewing, of all places, where the Chinese Communist Party had its historic roots? It was as if the revolutionary soil had held on to the peasants' vigilance only to come to life again after many decades because of new injustice.

Yan'an in Shaanxi has a similar historical significance. It was the village where in 1936 Mao Zedong and his supporters ended their legendary journey to escape the advancing government army. And it was there that Mao put on paper his most important political ideas and promised justice to the oppressed peasants: an end to the rigid power of large landownership and abolition of unjust agricultural levies.

It was all the more painful that sixty-five years later in that same area the peasants revolted about issues that looked suspiciously like the injustices that the Communist Party had battled in the past. Except this time the party turned out to be not a supporter of the peasants but an opponent.

In Zizhou, north of Yan'an and far from the reach of Beijing, officials of the local tax office had systematically squeezed money out of the peasant population in the area. This process had started in 1995 when new levies were imposed on the farmers from one day to the next. In addition to the then still compulsory agricultural tax, which according to the law was not allowed to be above 5 percent of the yearly income, all sorts of things were suddenly taxed. Feeding donkeys, cultivating apples, letting goats and sheep graze, training village militia, imprecisely defined retirement funds, drinking water, carrying out population politics, construction of highways, the army, township planning, specific products, and even the production of rain (the Chinese government sometimes shoots salt crystals into cloud banks in order to create rain)—money had to be handed over for everything.

"If we didn't pay, they would beat us up or seize all our household goods," said one of the victimized peasants. Most were no longer able to pay and daily begged for a meal from better-off peasants. This injustice continued for years. After two bad harvests and a summer of persistent drought, most peasants were fed up. In 1999 they decided to seek justice.

But the peasants were afraid of a violent confrontation with the local police. They knew that the police did not shun violence. That is why they turned to Ma Wenlin, a sixty-year-old high school teacher who since the early 1980s has been known for his legal defense of underprivileged and oppressed people in the region. "Ma is famous. If anyone was wronged, everyone knew where to find him," says Wang Xinwei, a journalist from Shaanxi television who followed and reported on the affair.

Ma, a self-made lawyer, needed very little time to consider. "Together with him, the peasants studied party documents and learned to use the law as a weapon in the battle against corruption," says Wang. In addition, Ma and the peasants felt strengthened by a recent legal precedent.

In 1997, the year when the farmers from Zizhou asked Ma for help for the first time, the peasants from the more northern village of Peijiawan, together with the regional law office of the district city Yulin, had managed to do the impossible. The twelve thousand peasants had accused the administration of their district of unreasonably high taxes and large-scale corruption. Each of them had placed his thumbprint under the charge.

With the help of lawyers from Yulin, the peasants had made use of a law that had come into force in the early 1990s; this law made it possible for the first time to lodge charges against Chinese officials. Despite this law, processes against the state had seldom ended in success.

But what happened? Contrary to everyone's expectations, the court of Yulin agreed with the peasants, and the tax bureau of the district where Peijiawan is located was ordered to cut the taxes in half.

At first Ma and the five thousand peasants from Zizhou and the surrounding area were successful, too. The abuses in the region were too numerous and the case seemed favorable. A national newspaper, the influential *Legal Daily*, in the article "Why Are the Taxes of the Peasants in Zizhou So Heavy?" gave Ma a whole page to plead his case.

Yet the peasants' petitions, which had been submitted to courts at several governmental levels in the province, were denied one after the other. "They told us that these [tax fraud] problems existed everywhere in the country," one of the peasants said later to a Hong Kong newspaper. "They said: 'If we take up your case, the party will have to do the same everywhere.' " And the local leaders, hardly a surprise, were just as fractious. "They said: '[Former president] Jiang Zemin is corrupt, all the leaders are corrupt; against whom do you think you're struggling?' " And that's how it was left.

After an official silence of several months, the affair suddenly started to get out of hand. Radical peasants from Laoshanmao, a village near Zizhou, took an official from the district government hostage. Of all people, this person was a bookkeeper on a reconciliation mission, but the peasants didn't care. They held him for six days.

The leaders in Zizhou were furious and intervened. They sent a police force to the village, tore the place apart, and arrested the peasant leaders of the petition movement. This seemed to have nipped the affair in the bud.

Nothing happened for a whole year.

But the frustration remained, and the peasants couldn't really believe that there was no higher authority in the province who would listen to their problems. Ma decided on a last, desperate try. He gathered the peasant leaders from eight communities under Zizhou to go to Beijing personally to submit a petition to the most senior leaders.

The peasants put all their money together, traveled to the capital together with Ma, and went to the State Bureau of Letters and Calls (Petition Bureau) in the southern part of the city. But the group from Zizhou hadn't been there even fifteen minutes—they were waiting their turn outside—when they were arrested, together with Ma.

This was the end of the mission. The peasant leaders were sent back to Zizhou, were arrested again on the spot, and were tried hurriedly. Some of them were condemned to eighteen months in prison. Ma was taken to court, too. He was accused of "rabble-rousing activity" as an accessory to the hostage taking of the previous year. One lawyer managed to get five witnesses to give evidence against the accused. Ma argued his own case, but to no avail. The judges had their verdict ready and condemned the self-made lawyer to a sentence of five years' forced labor.

One year later, in August 2000, the peasants of Zizhou were still furious. Thirty thousand of them, a quarter of the district's population, signed a petition addressed to the provincial court of Shaanxi. It was a plea to free Ma. But the defiant dynamism of the previous years seemed broken for good. Most of the peasants no longer had faith in it. "We are left to our own devices," one of them said gloomily.

SWALLOW OR LEAVE (Hubei, Jianli, Qipan)

In recent years several politicians and agricultural specialists have suggested replacing all agricultural levies in the country with an all-encompassing tax. This could abolish abuse once and for all.

It was an obvious but daring idea. The lowest government levels of China did not like it because it might threaten them with the loss of direct access to their most important sources of income. It turned out that the village, township, and district governments got practically all their income from levies imposed on the peasants. From that money they paid their own salaries and also had to finance infrastructure projects, schools, and hospitals. The officials were used to taxing the peasants more or less—most of the time more—according to their own needs.

The state created an investigative commission to experiment with a new tax system in the agricultural province of Anhui. It determined that in an average district in the province with a population of 1.1 million, the peasants paid 26 million yuan ($3.2 million) in agricultural taxes yearly. In other words, the peasants paid less than $3.60 per person. But it turned out that most of the district income consisted of "extra levies" amounting to a total of 80 million yuan ($1 million) per year. Therefore, the peasants in Huaiyan paid an average of 96 yuan ($11.90) every year. On the face of it, that's not very much, but in practice the peasants were using their last reserves. Most of them spent more than they earned per year.

To prevent a worsening of the situation—the Chinese government had meanwhile become aware of the explosive relations in the hinterland—the National People's Congress decided in the spring of 2001 to take the advice of the agricultural specialists and to experiment with a new tax system. In several districts in Anhui, all taxes at the lowest governmental levels were canceled in exchange for a new levy at the township or district level.

Prime Minister Wen Jiabao has meanwhile decided that the agricultural tax will have to be abolished completely after 2008. Then the peasants will no longer be burdened by the "three deductions" (for public funds, social security, and administration) and "five levies" (for education, family planning, military training, road building, and subsidies for special groups). This will cost the state about $15 million per year, but it would put an end to centuries of "disproportionate obligations," according to Minister of Finance Jin Renqing.

Chen Xiwen of the Central Leading Group of Financial and Economic Affairs of the State Council, who was responsible for the national agriculture policy, predicted in the beginning of 2005 that before the end of the year the 5 percent agricultural tax would be abolished in at least twenty-four of the thirty-one Chinese provinces. This would alleviate the existing inequality with the income in the city, because in the city income tax has to be paid starting at an income of $1,200 per year. But it is an important, chiefly symbolic, development. It is no longer difficult for the central government to be generous, because the national income from agricultural taxes has become negligible in recent years—evidence of how much the Chinese economy is changing. In 2003 that tax was only 1 percent of the national income.

The local administrations, where the rake-off from government money has traditionally been considerable, are not happy with it. They invent all sorts of regulations to generate money anyway. For example, several provinces have discovered the new houses of migrant peasants. Those modest dream homes are the most tangible proof of the money streaming from the city to the countryside. The government wants to enjoy that, too, and hence new houses are taxed more often.

But the province keeps complaining. "Township officials have heavy responsibilities," writes Gu Wenfeng in his book *Extraordinary Confessions*, published early in 2006. It is a book that is part of a new tradition of controversial charges, but this time it was written not by a peasant or someone sympathetic toward them but by an official and party chief from Hebi in Henan Province. "Most of the time we don't have the money or the right to fulfill [our responsibilities]—that is the crux of our difficulties," he writes. Many townships and districts are practically bankrupt because they can no longer cough up the salaries of the growing civil service corps. In 2004 this debt had supposedly reached $75 billion just at the village and township levels.

Gu does not justify the fact that practically all the municipalities and districts in China tried in recent years to pass these debts on to the peasants. But in a discussion with Reuters press agency, he asks for understanding. "Chairman Mao was right: the greatest hurdle that must be cleared is to inform the peasants adequately. Peasants are more aware of their rights—that is a good thing—but they treat officials as almighty, and we are not."

There were obvious reasons why this trimming of the expensive bureaucracy encountered much resistance. Xinhua, the official Chinese news agency, determined early in 2003 that in China one out of every twenty-eight Chinese was a government official. It would be necessary to call a halt to the ever-expanding bureaucracy. Administratively China had degenerated into a relief center for failed leaders of bankrupt state-owned enterprises, and the system was also terribly corrupt. With increasing frequency there were reports in the Chinese media that showed that the positions of village head, municipal bookkeeper, or district secretary were simply for sale for considerable sums.

To get rid of these problems, Prime Minister Wen promised the rural administrations a subsidy of $12 billion per year. It is a subsidy that is part of his New Socialist Countryside program. Public servant Gu was delighted. Although he applauded the proposal to abolish the agricultural tax, no one had paid attention to the bureaucrats, who would come under even more pressure. That would finally change.

But the countryside doesn't seem to be quieting down. If any actions are taken on behalf of the peasants, they don't go far enough for many, and above all they are coming too late. In addition, no one knows how the new regulations will be enforced. Peasants say that when Beijing sets its mind to implementing a new policy, many bureaucrats act as if they are listening. But when the storm has passed, the campaign ended, and the lessons learned, many of those bureaucrats simply pick up where they left off and continue doing what they have always done. The most desperate among the farmers protest or leave, and they do that en masse. In 2000 in Qipan, in Hubei Province, 65 percent of the fertile agricultural soil lay fallow because twenty-five thousand of the forty thousand inhabitants who originally lived in the township left their land out of sheer despair.

The situation in this area, which since the 1990s had been promoted as the new granary of Hubei and where only grains are allowed to be cultivated, was so worrisome that Li Changping, the township's party secretary, had dared to write a letter to the then Chinese prime minister, Zhu Rongji. His cry for help, which managed to circumvent the usual bureaucratic channels, must have made such a great impression that the letter actually landed on the desk of the prime minister and was published in its entirety in several national newspapers in the summer of 2000.

"The peasants are in great distress, agriculture is in danger," is how Li started his letter. He described how the peasants had left their land en masse in order to escape the money-hungry tax inspectors. This was why many peasants who stayed behind were condemned to begging. "I often meet older people who grab my hands and say that they hope to die soon," wrote Li, who was thirty-seven years old at the time. "And I see the sad eyes of the young children who fall down on their knees in front of me and beg me to be allowed to go to school again."

The situation that Li described in his letter was shocking and had seldom been made public in such a direct way by a party member. Moreover, the fact that Li himself was part of an administration that had failed so miserably in his eyes, but against which he no longer knew what to do, really hit home for the party officials.

"Party members at lower levels curry favor with the leaders, continually adjust the statistics, and pretend everything is all right," wrote Li. "Honesty is no longer rewarded. If someone tells the truth, he is immediately stigmatized as someone who is politically immature and unreliable."

Li made a long list of abuses and problems in Qipan. There, too, taxes were the greatest obstacle. Li reported that 80 percent of the peasants in his township had lost money. He wrote that 85 percent of the peasants still had savings in 1995, but now the same percentage was in debt. The average deficit of the village administrations in Qipan came to $60,000, and in most of the villages this debt increased by 20 percent per year, according to Li. It was not much better in the townships.

Li recounted that it was with pain in his heart that he had seen the peasants of his region leave. "In the past they left with a destination or a concrete job in mind. Now the peasants left hoping for a bit of luck and with the conviction that in a next life they wouldn't have to be peasants anymore." Li could understand these peasants. In the summer of 2000, he, too, handed in his resignation and settled in the growing city of Shenzhen. His situation in Qipan had become untenable when his colleagues accused him of treason after his cry for help had become public. Even the prime minister of China had been unable to protect him from the corrupt influence of the local party officials.

Lulu and Congcong feasting on ice cream and cake

Roses Wrapped in Plastic

Flower Peddlers
(Hunan, Changsha)

The little girl sounds cheerful: "If I have flowers left over, they beat me." She seems in good spirits and moves her hand in front of her face. "But I always sell everything," says the other girl. They giggle.

When most children are asleep, Cai Lulu and Yi Congcong start their day. That's when they are on the street, trying to sell their wrapped roses to the people who populate the bars and discos of Changsha until early in the morning. They hold the roses in front of them and in this manner waylay the strolling couples and the pairs of lovers. The girls know that they are eager to spend money. They insist until the irritated men finally give in and buy a flower to get rid of the badgering twosome and also not to lose face. No man wants to create the impression that his partner is not worth just one of these roses.

When they've gotten rid of all their roses, Cai and Yi go home. That's usually after midnight. If there still is a bus, they take it; otherwise they walk back—a walk of one and a half hours to a dimly lit, drab industrial district. It isn't until the early sunlight strikes the city that Cai and Yi fall asleep. They are exhausted. That's normal for girls of their age. They are six and eight years old.

• • •

Children selling flowers are to China what shoeshine boys are to Latin America; they can be found in all entertainment districts of the big cities in China. Changsha, the capital of Hunan Province, is even notorious for them. The land in the hills and around the lakes of Hunan is fertile and suitable for flower cultivation. Generations of Chinese in this region have lived off it. Yet there is poverty as well. To supplement the family income, the most desperate among the peasants send their children to the big city.

But when I am in Changsha, there is practically no child to be seen. While roaming the streets of Changsha for three long nights, I don't see the flower-selling children. They seem to be running away or are looking for the safe anonymity of the night.

The nightlife public is not sorry about that, because the pestering and peddling children are not beloved. "It's almost impossible to get rid of them," says Huang Ping, a journalist at a local television station. "One 'no' is not sufficient. They really persevere. If you continue to refuse, they practically pull your clothes off your body."

But where are the street children right now? Huang Ping has a suspicion. As an insider, she has heard about a much talked-about program that a competing Hunan television station showed a few days earlier. The report that was televised could be the reason that the children are not showing themselves right now. After all, it was about them. The controversial subject had never before been discussed in the local media. An enterprising journalist didn't want to ignore the question any longer and decided to depict the injustice being done to these children.

The report was televised, unleashed many reactions, and resulted in a genuine police roundup. People were arrested by the dozen and sent back to their villages. The young migrants and their parents or guardians who had avoided the police were very frightened and stayed out of sight just to be safe. Many growers and sellers sought shelter or left Changsha. "They are afraid to be arrested," says Huang Ping. And that fear was justified.

Jiang Jiamin, the journalist who made the documentary, was shocked by the effect of his work. He starts apologizing immediately. "I thought that this kind of social injustice could be discussed," he says, upset. After all, every Chinese journalist ought to know how far he can go. For enterprising reporters like Jiang, this means feeling his way to limits where others don't dare to go. This is the consequence of investigative journalism Chinese style, where censorship does not exist officially until tacit limits are overstepped. Jiang should have known to what risks he exposed his interviewees. He feels guilty about that.

But the harm had already been done. The documentary had barely been televised when the authorities contacted Jiang. "They wanted to know everything—addresses, names, backgrounds." He obeyed willingly. "What else could I do?" he says. Jiang was afraid of reprisals. So he had to stand by and watch the police immediately go into action. The families he had depicted were located without much trouble, then fined and sent back to their villages. After that a campaign was announced in Changsha to free the city once and for all from those "bothersome" street children and their "exploiting" migrant parents.

Jiang is particularly upset over what he has brought about because during the filming he had come to feel compassion for the people he saw in his viewfinder. "I wanted to show how adults exploit children. No more and no less. People who do that should be dealt with harshly." Those he found were not cruel wardens or heartless parents, but mostly loving and destitute fathers and mothers who were economically so down and out that they could no longer care for their children and had sent them into the street out of sheer poverty. "Actually, their children were better off in the street than at home," says Jiang. He felt sorry for the migrant families.

One of the unprocessed tapes of his report shows what he encountered in the abovementioned district of Changsha. The images of a lengthy report show Jiang finally tracking down the parents of the street children. There are drab districts, decayed streets, a garbage dump, and especially the questioning eyes of passersby. The digital camera, operated by Jiang himself, bounces up and down as he walks. The image stops in front of a weather-beaten door. The cameraman himself knocks. Then the door opens: The frightened eyes of a sleepy man with uncombed hair stare into the lens.

Nothing has been said yet, but it is clear that the man realizes immediately that catastrophe is at his door. Jiang asks his questions in a sharp tone. He sounds stern, and the camera records how Jiang's associates enter the house uninvited to the right and the left of the man.

The man is so intimidated that he mumbles his answers in a daze. He shows his identity card willingly. The camera zooms in on it. His name becomes visible, even his residence. Mr. Zhou from northeast Anhui is unmasked in front of the eye of the camera.

Then the lens shows the image behind frightened Zhou. There is a woman in a bed who looks frightened. She is not alone. Jiang's lens zooms in on the pile of blankets next to her, where a small girl is hiding behind the woman. Is it her daughter? The girl has colored braids in her hair and looks into the lens with big, confused eyes. In the corner of the room stands a small bucket with roses wrapped in plastic. You can hear Jiang think *Got you!* The flowers fill the screen triumphantly. The evil genius behind the flower children has been caught in the act.

Back with the adults, who turn out to be the parents of the little girl, a little boy also sticks his head out from under the blankets in the background. And another little girl appears from behind the mother.

Neighbors get to speak. They point accusingly in the direction of the flower seller's house and confirm the evil rumors. With their own eyes they have seen how the migrants sent their children out into the streets in the evening. How they put the flowers into plastic sleeves day in and day out. It was a disgrace. But what could they do about it?

• • •

Jiang offers to visit the people he filmed once more. It was a week ago that he was there for the shoot, and who knows, they may still be there. The taxi stops in a district called Malangdui. It is an old industrial district of Changsha that in reality is even more desolate, dusty, and dirty than Jiang's images conveyed.

Nothing in this neighborhood evokes any association with children. It's a godforsaken spot where no one would want to live. It is typical of the places where Chinese migrants end up most of the time: the bleakest, dirtiest, most dilapidated, and most unappealing districts of the city.

After several minutes the garbage dump from the film images comes into

Some children come to the same places so often that they know the customers. They remain watching at a distance until one of the diners finally buys a flower and, even more important, hands them the leftover food.

view—the same faces, the same surprised looks. But no one stays and stares this time. Most of them turn around quickly and walk away.

The weathered door appears once again. There's no need to knock, because a lock hangs on it. A bedridden neighbor, who wasn't able to get away, knows why. "Yesterday morning they left with the whole family and their belongings, back to Anhui," he says hoarsely.

Another neighbor woman has a key and opens the room. The space looks as if it had been hit by an earthquake. The bed stands untouched, but the floor is strewn with junk—pages from a school notebook with characters in a child's handwriting, everywhere wrapped red roses.

Neighbors who can't control their curiosity mumble amounts of fines, punishments, and destinations. The day after the broadcast of Jiang's report, the police searched the neighborhood thoroughly, and they haven't gotten over the scare yet. One person knows that all the family members, including the children, had to pay fines of 300 yuan ($37) per person. Another believes that they didn't pay anything ("They don't even have money!") and were put on the train home.

"The mother had six children; she was handicapped and couldn't do anything but put her children to work," volunteers one of the bystanders in defense of the driven-off peasants. He takes to his heels when he suddenly recognizes the journalist Jiang.

LAUGHING IN THE STREET

After long evenings of fruitless wandering through the narrow, wet streets of Changsha—it's been raining for more than a week—I'm suddenly face-to-face with two little girls carrying a bag filled with flowers: Cai Lulu and Yi Congcong. They look impudent and both immediately sell me a flower.

While eating an ice cream on the third floor of a quiet coffeehouse across from the entrance to a disco where they try to sell their wares, they are willing to talk. The girls, still very young, are ready for something nice to eat. The head of the smaller one, Congcong, barely sticks out above the table. Self-consciously, Lulu sits up straight. The two start to giggle. In very few words the little girls, who would be in the first and third grades in the United States, sum up the adult facts of their daily, or rather nightly, routine.

Every evening at around ten o'clock, Lulu and Congcong take the bus to-gether. They carry a plastic bag filled with flowers—that night's merchandise. Once they are downtown, they wander around the entertainment districts of Changsha looking for potential buyers of their wrapped roses—by then wilted packages. Lulu and Congcong go by the terraces, walk through the streets where masses of people are eating crawfish, a local specialty, in the open air, and wander around the mobile snack bars. There are many parading couples that are enjoying skewers with roasted beef or mutton, and, who knows, the girls may be able to get hold of a stick.

Each of the girls pushes a flower into the faces of potential buyers, pulls at sleeves, and follows anyone who seems to hesitate—until she has sold another flower or has begged a stick or a bite of something or other. In this way they fill their hungry bellies as the night wears on. Apparently they are good at it; both Lulu and Congcong look well fed.

Congcong asks if she may have a hamburger; Lulu wants a cola. They haven't even finished their ice cream yet. Lulu and Congcong understand the art of calculated but persistent nagging and whining. They stick up for each other.

Every day the two earn about $9. Half of the money goes to the woman who takes care of them. Lulu and Congcong call her *jiejie*, or older sister, but it's not clear how she is related to the children. The girls are allowed to keep the rest of the money, which is intended to finance their education. Lulu knows that they are returning to their parents in Anhui on September 1. That's when school starts for Congcong. It's now May, and it's not more than a promise from *jiejie*. Lulu and Congcong have been in Changsha for ten months, and they can only guess what the future has in store for them. It is *jiejie* who decides it.

"We're not real sisters," says Lulu, who is the older one; she laughs hard. "She is much meaner than I," says the younger one and pokes Lulu. "She scratched me," says Lulu again. "Here, here, and here." Then she suddenly says that her parents don't live in Changsha. "They worked in the fields. Now they have sold the land and are building houses." Congcong is disbelieving. "How can they just build houses?" Lulu answers, "Oh, yes, others give them food." Does this mean that her family is going hungry? The two are silent and stir their almost melted ice cream.

What does become clear is that the two girls had no say about being sent to the city. Lulu and Congcong were at school together until their parents decided one day to hand the raising of their preschoolers temporarily over to a woman who had apparently managed to convince them that their financial burden would be reduced if the little girls were put to work in the city. Lulu and Congcong give no hint of what they think of that, but they don't look very unhappy.

When Congcong returns from the toilet, she is crying. She has just discovered that she has lost 10 yuan ($1.25). She looks under the table but can't find anything. A little later she finds the missing money in her underpants. Both girls roar with laughter.

"One time a thief stole all my money," says Congcong when she stops laughing. It was 50 yuan ($6.20) from under her pillow. "He only stole change from me," Lulu adds. "I keep the big money someplace else." The girls share a bed in a room for the two of them.

Lulu and Congcong say that they live with six adults who are responsible for almost sixty children. The youngest of these children is four and the oldest is sixteen. Once in a while a two-year-old toddler comes along and is accompanied by one of the older children. According to the girls, they are well cared for by the adults. They don't want to say much more. It soon becomes evident that the girls have learned precisely what they can and can't say. And they stick to their script. They wouldn't dream of telling me where they live. And when they no longer feel like talking, they slip back into whining for sweets and

Customers may choose between a flower and a song. The songs are popular. The children sing out of tune and barely play the guitar, but the texts are obscene. People really like that when it comes from children.

drink. They play with sugar cubes, blow through straws, and stand on the chairs.

"I was on television," Congcong suddenly says proudly. "Filmed by the police." "By the police?" "Yes, when we were arrested." Congcong brags a little about her first television appearance, especially because Lulu says that she has never been filmed. She giggles and crawls under the table.

Then a coffeehouse server puts an end to the conversation. The girls have to leave. The woman has followed the conversation with the street children suspiciously from a distance and is worried. Officially there are no street children in Changsha.

When the girls hear that, they suddenly want to get rid of all their flowers. They have twenty with them and ask 5 yuan ($0.50) per flower. "If we don't sell all our flowers, we get a spanking," says Lulu pretend-pitifully.

"*Jiejie* likes nice clothes," she says suddenly. How does "sister" get the money for these nice clothes? "From us!" the girls shout. Finally the truth comes out. The girls have nothing left after their nightly strolls. When they come home at two o'clock in the morning, they empty their pockets under *jiejie*'s watchful eyes. Only then are they allowed to go to sleep.

"Sometimes I wake up at three in the afternoon. Then I go and play until I'm tired again," says Congcong. After that they get ready for the next working day. They eat a little rice, some vegetables, sometimes a bit of meat, and then set off for the city again.

When the girls have finished their ice cream, it is one o'clock in the morning. They are expected home in a few hours. Talking and joking, they walk outside without saying good-bye. Congcong lowers her underpants and pees quickly behind a tree. Then they cross the street, zigzagging through the busy traffic. Their slim bodies are lit up in the yellow headlights of an oncoming taxi. A bus at the other side of the road blocks the view for a moment. Then the girls suddenly disappear. Across the street there is not a trace of Lulu and Congcong.

Doctors and Soldiers

Education
(Beijing, Haidianqu)

Because it is 98.6 degrees Fahrenheit outside and it's scorching inside, the floor has been wetted down. The sandy concrete "splashes" with each step, and the children stand in the puddles in their plastic shoes or their bare feet. But the water barely cools the space. The schoolrooms look like shallow mud puddles, and there is a pungent smell of mold and sand in the air. The question is what is better, the imaginary cooling off or the stench.

The children don't care. Half of them are sleeping, and the other half are slumped over their school desks. They are four and five years old—not yet of school age. The teacher, called Miss Yu by the children, continues imperturbably with the lesson she started that day.

The children are taught the rudiments of the Chinese language. Not simple characters, but letters of the alphabet: *b*, *p*, *m*, and *f*—the first step that will help them later to pronounce and analyze characters. Sternly Miss Yu taps with her finger on the faded blackboard. *"Bo, po, mo, fo,"* she calls out after every tap. Five of the ten children in the lowest grade of Yujing, a school for migrant children, imitate her obediently and go down the list.

The sleeping children are shaken awake. Miss Yu prods here and there, but

While half of the class is busy with their homework, the other half receives instruction. Calmly the students continue working.

they are exhausted. She decides to leave them alone. "They're still too small," she says finally. "They should actually be at home and in bed, but their parents are on the streets in the city all day. Officially they don't have to go to school."

"Officially" is an elastic concept here. Headmaster Qin Xueling's school does what is necessary, but everything is done illegally. Most of the pupils reside without permission in the city where their parents have found work without permits, and therefore they have to attend an unlicensed school.

"Without us they can't go anywhere," explains Qin. Despite the nine-year compulsory school attendance that was introduced in 1986, the official schools in the city are open only to peasants with the proper permits. And they have to be wealthy enough to pay the extra-high tuition. That turns out to be a rare combination.

In some cities, the schools ask for a health certificate in addition to a residence permit and the parents' work permit. These permits and certificates are not always issued, and therefore many peasants get by without. In addition, all authorized schools charge special fees for peasants that vary depending on the school's level of aversion to the peasants. For example, schools in Beijing ask an average of 560 yuan ($70) tuition and 1,120 yuan ($140) "registration money." It's a lot of money, but many peasants can manage it. However, practically no peasant can pay the compulsory sponsor money, an arbitrary amount between 1,000 and 30,000 yuan ($3,700), which is dependent on the quality of the school and the disposition of those in charge.

Only the migrant workers—precisely the poorest section of the population—have to cough up this illegal levy. The migrants suspect that these fees were created to encourage them to stay away, and most of them do exactly that.

But not all migrants are resigned to this situation. "Education," says principal Qin, "is vitally important for the peasants. They want a better life for their children, especially because they themselves never went to school."

It is rather ironic. The peasants go to the city looking for a better income and a better life. But because they are practically without rights in the city, their children are usually worse off there than in the countryside. The schools in the countryside hardly make any distinction between origin and background, and the children get an education for a fixed amount of money. That advantage, however modest, also goes for other services, such as medical care and social services. In the countryside, all peasant sons and daughters are vaccinated against childhood diseases, but in the city they are deprived of these protections.

Yet this doesn't stop the peasants. On the contrary, more and more peasants take their children with them to the city, often because there are no family members who can look after the children at home in the village, or simply because the peasants don't want to break up the family. In this way almost all migrant children end up in illegal schools like principal Qin's, where conditions are perhaps not the best, but where most teachers—out of idealism and love of the profession—offer at least a basic education to thousands of children who would otherwise be condemned to the streets.

Teaching is in the Qins' blood. In his home province of Henan, Qin was already in front of a class. After coming to Beijing three years ago, he immediately started work as a teacher. "I can't do anything else," he says modestly. "I've taught all my life. It's the only thing I have learned."

That is also true for his wife and his child—they, too, are teachers. His wife teaches at a peasant school in the Qins' native village, his adult daughter at his own Yujing school in Beijing. Qin shares a small room with his daughter in one of the annexes of an old factory.

Father and daughter Qin get along very well with each other, joined in their common effort to offer a future to children who have few prospects. It is a rare collaboration that is striking in a land where ideals are scarce. But the Qins also came to the city because both have expectations about their own future that they can't fulfill in the countryside. "One day I want my own modern school," says Qin. For Qin's daughter, her work is her life, and she barely thinks about her own well-being. "I'm not complaining." She lacks the time for it.

Wang Yan, a new teacher at the school for migrants, is driven by ideals, just like the Qins. "I won't get rich here," she says. Money is not her motive. "But it gives satisfaction to teach these destitute children something." She means it. The young woman from Shijiazhuang is remarkably neat. She teaches the way she looks: The chapters from the exercise book are treated as thoroughly as her tightly plaited hair. Nothing betrays her meager existence.

The pupils are crazy about Miss Wang, even though she has been there only three days. The teaching material of that day consists of texts about moral values, a theme that is also treated at the regular schools in order to make the young people aware that they can help society and the party. The role model that Wang Yan quotes as an example is that of a self-sacrificing general. The children listen eagerly. When Wang asks a question, the children raise their

Thirteen-year-old Sun Xun is one of Wang Yan's pupils. He is enthusiastic and shouts his answers eagerly. At Yuying school he is a so-called "three good" pupil (*sanhao xuesheng*). He learns well, thinks well, and is healthy. The diploma that he received for those merits hangs above his proud parents' bed.

hands together as if bitten by a snake. And when Miss Wang nods, they answer out loud.

Yujing school is paid for by the peasant parents. For principal Qin, himself a migrant worker, that means compromise. Each of his hundred pupils— sometimes there are more and sometimes fewer ("Migrant workers are unreliable and leave from one day to the next")—pays $40 tuition per semester. But many parents, who earn an average of $130 per month, can't come up with that sum. Qin doesn't make an issue of it. "Those children may stay. That money will come one day," he says casually.

Because of this, his school contends with a structural lack of money. The school building, at the side of a dusty, unpaved road, is located in an old steel factory where heavy cables were formerly made. The several-yards-high sliding door through which the big rolls of steel cables used to be maneuvered into the large factory space is still used. Now there are thick brick walls in the large space, dividing it into three classrooms. There are no doors. They're not necessary, according to Qin. In the winter, heavy fabric hangs in the doorways to keep out the cold.

Because the classrooms can't be closed off, the classes shout over one another, but that doesn't matter, not even when the pupils shout loudly at their turn and rattle off their memorized lessons. There is a lot of shouting in Yujing school.

At home Sun Xun regularly helps his parents to spray water on the collected cardboard. That yields more money because wet cardboard is heavier. Sun Xun's father, who gathers the cardboard, comes from the same village as principal Qin. "Before he could go to school here, he was at a regular school," says Sun's mother. "That cost us a fortune. Qin was a godsend."

"I would like a better school for my pupils," says Qin, "but we don't have the money for it." For the time being he is happy that he still is where he is, but that can't be taken for granted. The building where he started his first school was lost to the wrecking ball because the district administration had decided that a drainage canal next to the school had to be widened. "Fortunately I hadn't put a lot of money into it," says Qin. He had watched resigned as the walls of the shed were torn down. It hadn't been much, and yet it was hard to bear. The move was relatively simple. The only things that belonged to him were the third-hand school desks and the well-thumbed schoolbooks, all of which fit into a good-size trailer.

Qin's new quarters are also a run-down building. He doesn't have much choice, since available space is scare. The old steel factory costs him a small fortune per year: 20,000 yuan ($2,480). With 4 million migrants in the capital, there is a good-size price tag even on a building due for demolition.

But Qin is more worried about the fact that he has no guarantee at all that his school can continue to exist intact. In the twilight zone where Qin and his colleagues operate, nothing is sure. For instance, in 2003 new rules were formulated that determine that you can start a school only if a contingency amount of 1 million yuan ($124,000) is in the bank, a sum that is out of the question for most migrant schools. All migrant schools that don't comply live with the threat that they could be closed at any time.

In recent years the migrants have already experienced a foretaste of massive closings several times. In the fall of 2001, 50 of the 200 migrant schools in Beijing were closed. In Shanghai 70 of the 519 schools were closed between 2001 and 2004—21 in one day.

Supposedly the schools were too dirty and too unsafe and were using poorly prepared teaching materials. But instead of offering an alternative to the migrant children, the city administrations left the forced closings at that. They did nothing else. The officials reasoned that safety came before schooling, and the pupils were simply turned out into the street. According to some estimates, this is the reason that in all of China, out of approximately 8 million school-age migrant children there are 1.8 million children who can't go to school.

In the migrant city of Shenzhen, 270,000 of the 456,000 children of school age were migrant children in 2002. But at least 100,000 of these 270,000 children were probably dependent on illegal schools like Qin's. The city administration calculated that in order to solve the problem of that shortage, fifty new schools would have to be built. Yet, despite the fact that the migrant society is vitally important to the economy of Shenzhen, the city administration is not prepared to put more money into the education of migrant children.

Several city administrators have expressed alarm because there are more and more migrant children. In Beijing the number of migrant children is increasing by 40 percent every year, according to the Chinese Ministry of Education. It was for that reason that in 2004 Beijing ordered all official schools to admit 240,000 of the 340,000 migrant children of the capital as an emergency measure. The year before, "only" 80,000 children were admitted.

But metropolitan schools as well as parents are beginning to complain about overcrowded classes. It seems that in Shijiazhuang, as in China's other big cities, classes of sixty to eighty pupils are no longer an exception, as revealed by an investigation of the local chapter of the All China Women's Federation.

Migrants who do have money at their disposal and want to set up a school are thwarted from all sides. They are not entitled to a subsidy, and the required permit needed to start a school can be obtained only in the villages and cities of origin, that is, in the peasants' hometowns, an impossibility, according to the principals of the migrant schools in the city. Therefore, the only thing left for them is to be illegal.

Many migrants are frustrated about their children's distressing school situation. An increasing number of Chinese who are politically involved with the question of the migrants or are studying it have warned about the explosive character of the problem. A 2001 study by the Chinese government found that "in young and sensitive minds [like those of the migrant children] rude treatment can cause permanent damage. Traumatic experiences can turn into hate and an aversion to life in the city when these children become adults. Without education the second generation [the migrant children] will grow up as illiterate lawbreakers."

The consequences of these concerns have also affected Yujing school. To give the impression that the city administration is somewhat concerned about the children of the migrants, various quality universities have been ordered to volunteer their services to the illegal migrant schools under a program called Project Candlelight. During our visit a second-year student of the Agricultural College in Beijing is teaching the highest grade—not agricultural techniques, but English.

The young man is inexperienced, his English is frankly lousy, but the children think it's terrific. "Me naime ees Zhang," the young man says loudly. "Ai aam Chineez." The children shout out after him. Zhang's comical accent is copied flawlessly and in unison. The small cassette recorder he has brought along is especially impressive. The children listen attentively, fascinated by the gadget. Then Zhang orders his pupils for the day to repeat the alphabet ten times. They do it obediently. No one seems to understand the simple sentences that Zhang reads out loud at the end of the lesson.

Apparently that doesn't matter. Principal Qin makes that clear once again when he leaves his class alone for a while to speak to his visitors. "We're not so exact," Qin says without shame. "It's nice that they're at least being taught." When he returns to his class, the children are still diligently doing their homework.

In an adjacent classroom, where thirty children's voices are once again shouting out a song, second and third graders are sitting together. When the children in the lower grade are doing their homework, the teacher turns to the right side of the class, where the older classmates are seated. The system works amazingly well, and the younger ones do their fill-in-the-blank exercises while the older ones noisily rattle off their memorized lessons.

Finally, as a playful exercise, each pupil may declare in one sentence what they want to become or what they want to experience. The children sound

No schoolbooks are as well thumbed as those of Yuying school. They are passed around; the children take turns using them. The most industrious among them copy the books for their younger brothers and sisters at home.

determined—there's no sign of the dissatisfaction that all the scholars warned about. One wants to become a doctor, another an inventor. Someone else wants to go into the army; his neighbor wants to be behind the steering wheel of a bus. There are at least three children who want to become painters, and there are two would-be chemists. They are hopeful children's wishes, and most likely none of them will come true as long as the existing separation between city and country persists.

When the lesson is almost finished, songs are sung just as in the morning: loudly shouted texts about Mao Zedong, the Chinese nation, and the army. Then the jangling noontime bell sounds; it is principal Qin banging a coal poker inside the sawed-off casing of an empty fire extinguisher. The children pour onto the square. They run, play with marbles, skip, and laugh a lot. It is ordinary children's fun at an extraordinary school.

KUNG FU AT DAYBREAK

Li Zhen, Father of Li Gen

The fact that their son has left the village has until now brought little good to the Lis. "He doesn't earn much," says fifty-two-year-old Li Zhen about his son. In the three years since he left, the younger Li has earned a maximum of $60 per month. His parents know that his place to sleep costs so much that he can send home almost none of his earnings.

Li Zhen (left) and his wife, parents of Li Gen

The older Li wouldn't mind working in the city himself because he can use the extra money. But he is needed in Shangdouyin. "We have a lot of land, 3.2 acres, and my wife can't manage that by herself." The peasants in this part of the country have more land than those in the south, "but the yield per *mu* is much lower. That's why we need a lot more land."

Li understands quite well why his boy works away from home. There is nothing more for him to do in Shangdouyin. "Let him go his own way," he says; "perhaps he'll find a wife."

Li Gen, Cook, Changping

Twenty-two-year-old Li Gen steams the buns and cooks the dumplings on a portable stove in the parking lot of the restaurant where he works. There are no cars in the lot yet because he starts cooking at three o'clock in the morning. It is an ungodly hour, when steaming buns in the open air seems

Li Gen

a rather senseless activity, but that is a misconception. The parking lot is filled with workers who have to start work early.

Li Gen doesn't enjoy his work very much. He looks tired in his grubby chef's jacket and hat. "You shouldn't do this work for too long," he reassures himself. It's clear that he has been doing it for too long. Just like his classmate Jianjun, Li Gen dreams of his own restaurant. When his alarm goes off at two thirty in the morning, he longs for home. It isn't until the morning sun shines on the parking lot and his working day is almost finished that he has time for himself. Then he huddles in front of the television and drifts off with cheap copies of Chinese kung fu movies.

"When I see Yu'er, I think of my own children. I have never given as much time to my own children as I've given her. There was no opportunity for it," says Suzhen. "Sometimes that makes me feel bitter."

Trust to the Threshold

Caregivers
(Shanghai)

According to the conventional wisdom of Chinese caregivers, the person who takes care of the child loves the child more than the biological mother does. It is said that only love that is greater than a mother's love can dispel the agitation of a child who misses his or her parents. But according to forty-nine-year-old Li Suzhen, nanny of seventeen-month-old Yu'er, that problem doesn't exist in this case because Yu'er doesn't even get the chance to miss her parents: They are never there. "Sometimes I wonder why Sun Lei and Yu Peigang have a child," she says about Yu'er's twenty-nine-year-old mother and thirty-three-year-old father. "In the morning they say hello in passing, and when they come home in the evening, their baby is already asleep. They never see their daughter."

But Suzhen has no say in this, and therefore she holds her tongue. Moreover, she can't blame Yu'er's hardworking parents. The baby is her livelihood, and the irony of the situation has not escaped her, for Suzhen is a mother herself. She has two daughters and a son who undoubtedly need her a lot. But she works almost every day of the year, far away from her brood.

This situation is not exceptional. Very many Chinese live far away from their

None of the migrant women who are waiting for employers in the municipal job exchange satisfy all of old Yu's specific requirements. He goes through the registration forms of other possible candidates while the director calls everyone old Yu points at. The atmosphere is relaxed, almost giggly—caused by nervousness. Many of the women are fed up with waiting and want to start working quickly.

families. Loved ones separate when it is necessary; parents leave their children behind with grandparents when duty calls, as if it were a matter of course.

Among migrant workers it is the most normal thing in the world to break up family life any time opportunities beckon, even if far away from home. This is also true for Suzhen. Her life is a succession of good-byes. But anyone who dares to say that Suzhen's children are not dear to her will feel her anger.

It's for a good reason that Suzhen does her work with a child that is not hers, in a family that gives her little freedom, in a city where she knows hardly anyone, far away from the countryside where she grew up. She does it for the future of her own children—so that they can go to school, perhaps even to the university, and thus can look forward to the kind of life that she herself never had.

This desire is perhaps self-evident, for what parent doesn't wish for a better future for his or her child? An obvious question comes to mind: Does the pain of being apart compensate for the uncertain future awaiting her children? Suzhen claims that it does.

A NIGHT'S REST

When I meet Li Suzhen, the household of Sun and her husband, Yu, is in a commotion. The kitchen help has just left, and Yu senior, Yu'er's grandfather, is worried. Apparently no food will appear on the table without kitchen help because old Yu is very busy with his wife, who is ill in bed. His son and daughter are at work all day, and Suzhen is permanently busy with Yu'er.

Yu senior is therefore looking for new kitchen help. It appears not to be easy, for sixty-seven-year-old grandfather Yu is choosy. The help should not be too young, should be able to cook well—if possible Jiangsu or Subei cuisine—and should have her own housing. "The previous kitchen help lived with us, but we couldn't have that. She slept in one bed with Suzhen, Yu'er's nanny, who was bothered by her snoring."

For his mission, old Yu hurries over to the local employment office of the Puta district in Shanghai, a small office on a busy street next to an aluminum-window-frame maker. There he sits down among roughly twenty nervously giggling women, all of whom are looking for work. They wait there all day long for employers, just like Yu, but none of them seem to have their own housing, and most cook Sichuan style, the spicy cuisine of the province where most migrant workers in this area come from.

Yu looks in a plastic folder containing the registration forms with photos of additional peasant women who are looking for work. He chooses several rosy peasant faces, and a friendly employee of the municipal job exchange tries to reach them. To talk on the phone, she has to raise her voice whenever the electric saw of her neighbors cuts the aluminum. But it is to no avail. The only mi-

The daily walks with Yu'er are a respite for Suzhen. Those are the moments of the day that she speaks with people outside Yu'er's family. "I really love this park," she says. The smell of the green in the city makes her long for home.

grant worker who showed any interest says on the telephone that she first wants to discuss it with her husband. In addition, her health has to be tested. That is a requirement of the Yus. The family wants written proof of the physical well-being of any peasant woman who comes to work in their house. "That's very normal," says Yu. "You don't want to expose your family intentionally to strange diseases." So the old man returns home without accomplishing his mission. Cooking will be Suzhen's responsibility this evening.

During a quiet moment when the whole family has left the house and Yu'er is sleeping in her arms, the usually quiet Suzhen carefully expresses her frustrations about the Yu family. They are too critical, breathe down her neck, and needlessly let go one kitchen help after the other—none of them last. Suzhen has seen four of them come and go. "The last one wasn't too bad," she says. She had been there for just a few days and promptly announced that she'd have to give notice the next day. There were "problems at home"—*jiali you shi*—a permissible reason that almost everyone in China gets away with when they don't feel like doing something for whatever reason.

The kitchen help had not said anything to Suzhen, either, but the latter didn't need many words to understand what was up; she didn't have it to her liking at the Yus. Therefore, the family is now without kitchen help, and Suzhen temporarily has an extra task. But at least she has her night's rest back again.

The day that Suzhen arrived in Shanghai for the first time, she did nothing but cry. She felt utterly miserable, even though things went well for her. "No more than two hours after registering with a job exchange, I got one." Suzhen started her career in Shanghai as an old lady's helper. "I helped her to go to the toilet; I washed her; it was not nice work." When the woman died and Suzhen was out on the street from one day to the next, she returned to her native region in Anhui.

But the situation there wasn't exactly rosy either. "The factory where my husband worked had gone bankrupt, and he was sitting at home, bored. I tried to convince him to look for work, but he doesn't listen to me."

Therefore Suzhen turned right around. "It's easier for women to find work than for men," she says in justifying the decision she made at that time. "In addition men spend much more money, even though they earn more. They smoke, drink, gamble, and before you know it everything is gone." Suzhen is different. She is thrifty, very thrifty, because she sends home almost all the money she earns. "More is left over of my monthly 800 yuan [$100] than of the 2,000 yuan [$250] that he used to earn," she says matter-of-factly. "In our village it's the men who stay behind and the women who set out."

The women from Anhui who end up in Shanghai find work without much trouble—usually as nannies. It is tiring but simple work. Most of them live with their employers and therefore don't have to worry about housing. Although their income is usually low, the flow of money is usually steady.

"I do almost everything," says Suzhen. She is an energetic woman, and except for her accent, nothing reveals her peasant background.

But she knows her place in the Yu family. Suzhen, who in the past few days has also been functioning as the cook, eats separately from the family. She says it's a solution to a space problem, but the temporary segregation in the small family is nevertheless distressing. Although the only grandchild, the pride of the family, knows Suzhen better than she knows anyone else, her nanny's place is on a chair in the adjacent bedroom, while the family eats at the table in the hall next to the kitchen. All of a sudden Suzhen, the woman whom little Yu'er trusts so completely, is a stranger to the Yu family.

"They are very good to me," Suzhen says without passion. "I can't complain." But then she reconsiders. "I wake up with the baby; we sleep together. It isn't until I have washed her, brushed her teeth, dressed and fed her that I can take care of myself"—that is, when old Yu and his wife are at home. If they are not, then Suzhen doesn't get around to taking care of herself. "Then I don't go to the toilet until Yu'er's afternoon nap. I can't leave her alone, can I?"

But even the baby's afternoon nap is no assurance of rest and relief. "Usually I cradle her in my arms and never let go of her; that way she sleeps longer." Then Suzhen leans her tired head against the green-painted wall for a moment to catch up on sleep, for the nights are tiring, too. "I'm the one who gives her a bottle at night." When Suzhen is ill, she simply continues working. "I can't do otherwise." And when the baby goes to the day care center on weekends, Suzhen has to go with her. "Her parents are afraid that she'll feel lonely there."

In short, Suzhen never has a moment for herself. "It's difficult work," she says finally. "If something happens to Yu'er, I'll get a scolding." That's why she is scared to death to leave the baby alone.

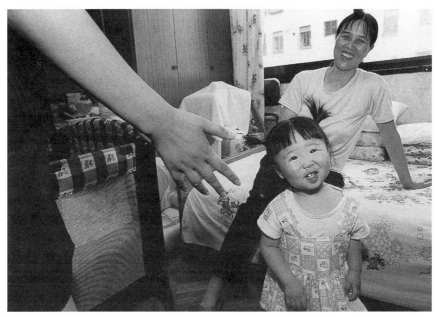

Every time Sun Lei (little Yu'er's mother) leaves, it's a small drama. But Suzhen is relieved when she's gone. Suzhen is busy with the little girl every day, but when one of the parents is at home she feels superfluous, intrusive, as if it's Sun Lei and not she who is raising Yu'er.

According to Suzhen, the Yu family is always worried about her so-called lack of understanding of hygiene. Undeservedly so, she thinks. "Doing laundry in the countryside is no different from doing laundry in the city. Peasants are not dirty by definition!" Moreover, grandfather Yu's frequent and noisy spitting seems to show that hygiene is a relative notion in this Shanghai family.

In the long run, she would like to leave, certainly when the family moves to a larger apartment. They are already planning it. "In a large house the chance for accidents is much greater." As it turns out, says Suzhen, the care of the aged, her first job in Shanghai, wasn't so bad. "At least you get a night's rest."

ALWAYS SEPARATED

"My children simply slept when I wanted them to," says Suzhen. "I call them once a week," she says. She misses her children and cries. "My oldest daughter of seventeen listens to me." But one and a half years ago, when Suzhen put her daughter on the train to Guangzhou, she wasn't at ease until the girl was with her classmates. "They all work in the same factory." Suzhen would have preferred her daughter to stay home, but she nevertheless encouraged her to go. "She now earns 1,900 yuan [$235] per month and rents a room with a girlfriend. She is independent and is better off than at home," she says firmly.

Suzhen believes that her youngest daughter has a good chance of being admitted to the university. She beams with pride when she casually discloses that her child is the second-best pupil in her class. "If she gets to the university, she'll be the first in the family. I went to school for only four years. That was because of the Cultural Revolution," when all education was stopped. The idea that a better future is awaiting her children motivates Suzhen to continue what she is doing.

"Every year we need 4,400 yuan [$445] for the education of my two youngest children." The $100 that Suzhen earns monthly in the employ of the Yu family is much needed. "In Anhui I earn 50 yuan less per month," she says. Fifty yuan? Did Suzhen leave her family for an extra $6.20?

The margins that cause the peasants to migrate to the city are narrow, but they turn out to be crucial in taking steps that would be called radical in the West. A few $10 bills are enough of a reason for Suzhen to be away from home for years.

The one time that she goes home—once a year around New Year's—serves above all a concrete goal: to bring money. The last time that Suzhen returned to Leqiancun in Anhui, she had 2,200 yuan ($272) in her suitcase. She was not afraid to travel with so much money. "I know the driver of the bus company; he comes from our village and I have his telephone number."

The seven-hour trip from Shanghai to Qianxizhen goes from progress and modernization, the most modern that China has to offer, to deprivation and relative poverty, the image that defines the Chinese hinterland. In the district that Suzhen comes from, migrants like her are the motor that keeps the economy running. There is not a family without a member who has been living and working for a long time outside the region. Among fellow villagers, Suzhen is no exception.

For the population of Leqiancun, Shanghai is the work destination of choice. "It's close by," Suzhen explains of the constant outflow from her village to the seaport, "and the food is better." It is an often recurring reason among migrants: We'd like to be anywhere, as long as the food is good. "That's why I would never want to go to Beijing. It's too far away and they don't know how to cook there."

Back in her village, Suzhen is often asked for help. Her experience in the city is considered successful for a woman of her age. "Most of the people who have stayed behind in our village look up to me," says Suzhen. "They envy me and ask me to put them in touch with employers in Shanghai, but what can I do?" Sometimes she feels obliged to help, especially when it concerns family members. During a previous visit in her village, two sisters-in-law came to her and asked whether she could arrange jobs for them. Suzhen couldn't refuse and showed them the way during their first days in Shanghai. "I introduced them at a hospital where I had contacts, and they even found work there," Suzhen says proudly. She had been very nervous about it for days. What if she had not been able to help them?

When six months later, during a visit to her village, some "family members" again came to her, Suzhen refused for the first time. After all, she was not a job agency and was happy to have her own job. She had no formula for the secret of her success. Her "family members" were offended and turned to someone else.

"Maybe it's because I'm used to taking care of myself," says Suzhen. She has done so since she was eighteen, when her husband, to whom she had just been married, left for a distant workplace without much warning. "We got married and immediately parted. I was very young; it made no difference to me." From her marriage in 1977 until a few years ago, she lived separated from her husband. "We have been together just since 1995," says Suzhen. That was the year she moved from her village to the nearby district city, the new workplace of her husband, who was recently laid off.

She doesn't have good memories of the reunion. After being separated for many years, living with the man to whom she had already been married for eighteen years was not easy. "There were many problems and we quarreled almost daily," she says. But they did not blame each other. "I'm never really angry at him. He is good to me. Also to our children, although they prefer to be with me rather than with him."

She liked the transition from the agricultural countryside to the district city where her husband had found a job in a cement factory. "I was especially happy for my children. After all, education is much better in the city." To legalize their status in the city and to make access to better schools possible, Suzhen paid for residence permits. They cost her well over 10,000 yuan ($1,240). But she didn't mind. "After all, there are more opportunities in the city."

Suzhen never considered a permanent move to Shanghai. That is too far from home. She doesn't feel at home there, especially for practical reasons. "The money that we earn in the country is gone very quickly in the city," she says. The money that she earns in the city goes farther in the country. "At home living costs are much cheaper. In the city everything is expensive."

But there is another reason that Suzhen doesn't long for the city. It's people like the Yu family, her employers. "Whatever I do, ultimately they don't trust me anyway," she says. How is she so sure about that? "When they aren't home, I'm not allowed to leave the house." According to the Yus, that is because it's pleasant and practical to have someone open the door when they return home. "But why is the door always locked?" Suzhen asks indignantly. They never gave her a key, and as far as she is concerned, the Yus' trust in her stops at the threshold of their front door.

A GUARD'S MARRIAGE PROSPECTS

Feng Bing and Li Shenghua, Parents of Yingcang

"Feng Yingcang was always lazy," says his father, fifty-one-year-old Feng Bing. "He didn't do his best at school and he never helped in the fields." Feng senior laughs about it. His son is out of the house, and that can lead only to improvement. "He thinks that you have to work too hard in the fields. Probably he has more time for himself in the city. In the countryside he can't raise hell." But the guard's work doesn't appeal to the father.

Do the old and the young Feng stay in touch? "Once in a while, by telephone. He asks about us; we ask about him. Most of the time he says that things are going well, and then we hang up again. We don't talk for more than a minute. Calling costs money."

The few times that Yingcang returns home, he sneers at the peasant's life. It doesn't bother his parents. "I can understand it," says Feng senior. "Country life is not very exciting." But the Fengs would never want to go to the city. Mother Li Shenghua, forty-six years old, who has never been in a city, fears the noise. She has heard about it from friends. Feng Bing, who is better traveled than his wife, didn't care much for it. "My place is here in Shangdouyin."

Feng Yingcang, Guard, Changping

Feng Yingcang, a twenty-two-year-old from Shangdouyin, is the only one of his male classmates who has a girlfriend. His friends say that he is lucky, for his position is not that great. Like his classmate Wang Sujun, he is a guard who oversees "public safety." His task is to watch who goes in and who goes out, nothing more. "Inside" is the language institute of the University for Politics and Law in Changping.

Feng Yingcang acts shy. He knows that he's lucky. In a world where young women have much more choice in love than young men because there are more boys than girls among the peasants, income plays an important role. In other words, guards don't have great marriage prospects.

Feng Bing and Li Shenghua, parents of Feng Yingcang

Many sons of peasants have left Shangdouyin because they believe that they will be more attractive to a woman if they have a job in the city—bet-

Feng Yingcang

ter to be a guard than a peasant. But Yingcang is an exception. He doesn't want to stay in Changping at all. In the long run he wants to return to Shangdouyin, and his girlfriend approves.

"First I worked in the building trade, but in the winter the work stopped and I earned nothing. Then I was gardener for the municipal public garden service for a while. After that the language institute hired me. This work is not as heavy, but it pays too little. All in all, I find life in the city difficult. You have to fight to survive. In the countryside, life is orderly; once a year you sow, then you harvest. In between you have time for yourself."

Yingcang works from six until six. Sometimes he stands, and sometimes he sits. Most of the time he is bored. "I long for Shangdouyin."

The Affair of the Cut-off Tongue

Justice

(Shanxi, Lanxian, Peijiazhuang)

Never before had the villagers of Peijiazhuang experienced such energy. In three days and three nights, construction workers who had been hired by the local administration of the impoverished peasant district built a new school in the village—three classrooms and a teachers' room. The construction workers were so rushed by the foremen that the stucco was daubed too thickly against the outside walls and oozed off on all sides.

For the four hundred inhabitants of Peijiazhuang, the construction of the new school was no reason for gratitude or joy. On the contrary, for them the gray building on an excavated slope was a symbol of the sad outcome of the personal crusade of one of them against an unreasonable, corrupt, and ultimately violent district administration.

The story of the school of Peijiazhuang is the story of Li Lüsong, a twenty-year-old country boy who, against his better judgment, entered into a struggle with the administration of Lanxian, a district on the loess plateau of Shanxi in central China. For years Lüsong had dedicated himself to getting a new village school built. The old school was so dilapidated that it almost collapsed, and Lüsong, a clever farmer's son who had finished high school, was of the opinion that the village of Peijiazhuang had a right to the financial support that had been promised. He sent a petition to the district but was rebuffed.

Disappointed but convinced that he was in the right, he made another attempt a few weeks later, and his petition was again denied. The young man wrote once again. Again his petition was refused. This process was repeated so often that in two years' time Lüsong had written a stack of petitions and protests that was almost two feet high. His fellow villagers called Lüsong honest and sincere, but as stubborn as a mule.

The administrators in Lanxian were unyielding. They were fed up with the country boy. When he ventured again onto the grounds of the Bureau of Education in December of 1999, the administrators grabbed the young man by the scruff of the neck and threw him roughly back into the street.

"I was furious," Lüsong said later to a Chinese journalist. "I went out and bought a can of red paint and at night I plastered the wall with slogans. I wrote: 'Ban corruption, ban corrupt administrators!' " Two days later he was arrested. The deputy head of police intervened in person. Lüsong resisted and in a fit of rage knocked off the police chief's glasses. The police chief answered with a wooden club and knocked the young man unconscious.

What happened in the following days, until the moment five weeks later when Lüsong's father was ordered to pick up his son from a hospital, was so horrifying that the district administration was banned from speaking about it by higher authorities.

Li senior, back from a construction job in the provincial capital Taiyuan, found his son half dead. He was fifty-five pounds lighter than when his father had last seen him and was black and blue all over his body. His ankles were black from the shackles that he had worn all those weeks, and the flesh of his heels had been scraped off so that the bone was visible. But much more shocking was the fact that Lüsong's tongue was half an inch shorter—cut off with a pair of nippers.

· · ·

The United Nations Committee Against Torture has more than once found China guilty of police cruelty. According to the committee, Beijing has in recent years made progress in specific areas of legal reforms, such as the assurance it has given that the international treaty against torture has to be enforced at all administrative levels, but at the same time it maintains a system that paves the way for police violence. So-called administrative detention is an example of this. This form of punishment gives the police the opportunity to lock up suspected persons for an indeterminate time or to send them to a labor camp without cause, legal hearing, or trial. It is a license for abuse.

The Chinese government recognizes the problem but is of two minds. Many human rights violations that take place in China are the result not of national policy but of local abuse, abuse that often goes unnoticed because it takes place outside the mainstream, in the countryside, in the villages, in hard-to-reach places. China would like to focus attention on it (since early 2004 an intellectual discussion has been taking place about the partial closing of labor camps) but knows that with more openness it will expose itself to criticism from the international community.

Yet, in the past few years, the president of China's highest court has publicly given a report about the existence of police abuse during the yearly sitting of the National People's Congress. In this way, the court has admitted that obtaining confessions by means of torture occurs most certainly. According to Chinese data, in the mid-1990s an average of 240 police interrogations led to the death of a suspect. Early in 2004, the Chinese press agency Xinhua published a report from China's most senior judge, Xiao Yang, finding that after extensive investigation, almost eight thousand prisoners who had been imprisoned too long or wrongfully were freed.

The investigation into the Lüsong case, which in the newspapers in China that dared to write about it (there were strikingly many) was called the "affair of the cut-off tongue," is typical of the difficulty that China has with openness in dealing with local human rights violations. Chinese newspapers more and more often feel called upon to break the "bad news is no news" tradition and expose corruption—which usually causes the peasants to come off worst—in no uncertain terms. The local police, who have been allowed to behave lawlessly for a long time, are increasingly getting caught, while the central authority watches uncomfortably as its own legitimacy is being undermined.

The story of Lüsong, the young peasant, got so much attention from the local media that the Lanxian police decided to mount a counterattack. They invited journalists from the *Police Daily*, a national newspaper of the Ministry of Public Security, in order to get the truth out in the open. The journalists of that paper concluded that Lüsong had himself to thank for his injuries. "We talked to his father for five hours," they wrote, "but Li Lüsong, who was lying right there, said nothing. When I asked him to open his mouth I saw a small wound. As if he had bitten his tongue."

In the spring of 2000, at the moment that I visited the police hospital in the city of Lishi where Lüsong was put up, father and son had just been moved elsewhere by the Lanxian district authorities. Upon inquiry we found that they were moved because of "safety concerns"—their location is unknown. Roommates of Lüsong, who had come into contact with the young man and his father, were furious about the report in the *Police Daily* in which the "affair of the cut-off tongue" was dismissed as a fabrication. "Is confirmation still needed?" one of the patients said angrily. "Those Lis are like this!" He gave a thumbs-up.

One hundred ten miles away, in their smoky farmhouse, Lüsong's family first reacts stoically, as if they have completely accepted their peasants' existence without rights and are resigned to the situation. But nothing is farther from the truth.

The stoic looks of the uncles and aunts who stayed behind in the village cannot disguise the fact that the family has unanimously set out not to be kicked around. "This is a family catastrophe," says one of Lüsong's aunts. "It doesn't just concern Lüsong and his father; it's as if all of us had our tongues cut off," she says bitterly.

Of course they think that cousin Lüsong is stubborn. " 'There is no point to it,' I told him regularly. 'Give it up!' " But then he'd again ride on a tractor, two hours over unpaved streets, "to protest in Lanxian." All of Peijiazhuang thought that Lüsong was unwise. No one had ever started a fight with administrators; it seemed risky. "And he doesn't even have children himself!" But when the news of Lüsong's mistreatment reached the village, everyone's blood was boiling.

The family made preparations and got support from the whole village. Now they want to press charges against the police chief of Lanxian. And if they don't win their case, they will continue to litigate to the highest level of China's judicial system. "We are selling our house. We're ready. If necessary we'll go to Beijing," says Lüsong's aunt.

The family knows that the school finally was built as a result of all the publicity. "To clear their conscience they've corrected their mistake hastily. But we won't rest as long as Lüsong has not received compensation."

Some progressive Chinese thinkers believe that the abuses won't be that bad in the countryside (and in the city) when the peasants become more involved in the local administration. If the peasants of Peijiazhuang had truly meaningful popular representation, then they could have raised their concerns formally with the Lanxian district administration. Lanxian in turn would have had to justify to the population the reason district policy—building a school—had not yet been carried out. Administrative negligence or more serious matters, such as corruption and assault, would have been made public and been punished harshly. But everyone in China knows that such an extent of participation is far from realistic. That is why most people hold their tongues. It's safer.

Yet China has been experimenting with a form of democracy since 1987. At the lowest administrative levels in the countryside and in the city, peasants and city dwellers may choose their own village heads and representatives. In more than eight hundred thousand villages, in sixteen provinces and autonomous regions, and in twenty cities, the population goes to the polls once every three years. Between 400 million and 700 million voters—Chinese statistics don't tally—have in this way been involved in the democratic process.

The Chinese media speak regularly of the peasants' enormous enthusiasm about elections. Everywhere in China they seem to have been involved in the daily goings-on in their villages, have outlawed corruption and abuse of power, and, even more important, have managed to make public funds flow back into society.

The English-language *Chinese Daily*, which regularly responds to the preferences of its foreign readers, who are more interested in the village elections than the Chinese public is, reported in the fall of 2002 that Beijing University had just concluded a study of the peasant democracy. The young researchers found that the "democratic consciousness of peasants is often much higher than among many of our fellow students."

"Democracy is spreading and has caught on in the countryside," says Wang Zhenyao, the assistant director of the Division of Village Democracy of the Ministry of Civic Affairs; he is delighted. His ministry is responsible for the introduction of elections at the village level. And Cai Dingjian, a member of the National People's Congress, expresses what according to him is the most important reason for holding elections: "It is good for the development of the economy." According to advocates of the elections, peasant participation in several regions has shown that economic prosperity has indeed increased.

But the question is whether peasants with their votes can actually exert influence or expose abuses. "The election system is set up to get more control over society—not to grant the peasants more freedom," says Yu Jianrong, an influential sociologist who has done much research on Chinese village democracy. He explains how the desire for village elections originated. "The party felt the need to restore its influence in the villages." With the collapse of the people's communes at the end of the 1970s, the local administrative structure also disappeared. Scarcely any taxes were collected, maintenance of the irrigation system was no longer carried out, and less and less money was available for collective services such as education and medical care. Village democracy had to turn this process around.

But it has not been easy up to now. Since the introduction of local elections, unrest in the countryside has increased, and there is little to indicate that the central government has the situation under tight control. Peasant uprisings take place all the time, and abuses like those of Li Lüsong in Peijiazhuang are the rule rather than the exception, a good reason for many peasants to leave the countryside for the city on the assumption that it is better there.

The party leadership is sharply divided about the value of village democracy. According to the old Communist guard, democracy is extremely dangerous, even at the village level. They feel that unskilled peasants must never get hold of a potentially explosive instrument like direct elections. Scholars with a more Western outlook don't agree; they believe in village democracy, as long as it is not abused by the district administrations. Such manipulation is not hard to imagine. Many districts try to control the elections.

A good example of unsuccessful countryside democracy is in Qianjiang in Hubei, which was described in detail in the south Chinese and Hong Kong press. In 1999, Qianjiang, a township of 354 villages, was proclaimed a Red Flag township, a mark of Communist recognition because the township elections in the previous ten years had supposedly been exemplary. Qianjiang was a township that all of China could learn from.

But appearances deceive. Things didn't go so perfectly in Qianjiang. This state of affairs was first determined by a retired teacher and an active member of a village committee in the township, Yan Qingjin and Yao Lifa. Urged on by dissatisfied villagers, they carried out independent research about the process of the elections in their township. They visited all 354 villages and talked with angry administrators and peasants.

It was found that 187 of the elected village heads had been removed from their functions under pressure from above and had been replaced by party faithful. It turned out that only a small percentage of all elections in the township had been carried out democratically. A village head who was clearly not liked by local party administrators was even removed from his function four times and was reelected again and again.

"When the party leadership says you have to go, then you go. Whether you were elected or not," says Yao with reference to the issue in the Chinese paper *Southern Weekly*. "If Qianjiang is a model township, then you can imagine what it is like in the problem regions." Their study attracted the attention of the provincial authorities of Hubei, who in turn brought it to the attention of the central administration in Beijing. There Yao's findings were published in internal party documents. But it did not help much. Despite multiple reprimands from the powers that be, the local administration was determined to ruin the lives of the two whistle-blowers.

The Chinese government does not like openness, especially not when that openness brings to light abuses like the ones that occurred for many years in Qianjiang. This is another reason democracy is difficult. After all, elections and openness go hand in hand. At the village level, this means that corrupt or incompetent party bureaucrats in particular resist elections. They don't want to be voted out and fear being unmasked by candidates who are no longer intimidated by the party.

Yao and Yan found that the elected village heads of Qianjiang were sometimes removed from their positions with brute force. In the model township, abuse turned out not to be rare. The party officials apparently assumed that most candidates would in the end remain quiet.

That was a misconception. On behalf of the aggrieved peasants, Yao and Yan struck back. Their first collision with the township was as a result of a tax campaign that got out of hand in Dongtan, one of the villages in Qianjiang. In the spring of 2000, the district administration sent tax inspectors to the village in order to make up the fast-dwindling township funds. The inspectors were assisted by gangs of thugs whose members were, if necessary, willing to teach a lesson to uncooperative peasants in exchange for $4.80, a carton of cigarettes, a toothbrush, and a towel.

A lot of resistance had been predicted, and the visit went as expected: At least nineteen villagers got a beating, were hauled in, and were condemned to "reeducation through labor"—a Chinese term for imprisonment. One of the condemned peasants was Zeng Xiangjun. Zeng was picked up because he was known as a troublemaker, not because he had refused to pay his taxes but because he had dared to make an issue of the existing tuition levy. Zeng had delved into the rules and had found out that collecting tuition was not allowed.

Zeng was behind bars for days, but after being freed he immediately approached Yan, the retired teacher. Yan, alarmed by the story, immediately set out to investigate. Together with Yao, he managed to get publicity for his findings about the "tax roundup" without much difficulty. The party secretary of Qianjiang, a powerful man, was apparently impressed by the story and let the involved officials "criticize." But none of the guilty were prosecuted.

Yan and Yao were not satisfied with that result. They delved deeper into the bookkeeping of Dongtan and came across many more illegal practices. For example, the pair discovered that large-scale voting fraud had been committed. During the elections of the previous year, one man had been credited with producing one hundred votes.

Once again the two brought the results of their investigation to the attention of the township. But this time they also made a demand: New elections had to take place. To everyone's surprise, they did take place—in January 2001. It was a great victory for Yan and Yao and for the villagers of Dongtan.

But things went wrong once again. The result of the elections was, as expected, clearly in favor of the villagers, but the township didn't like that. The elections were immediately declared to be invalid. With the support of the township, a new village committee was installed, which, as usual, consisted of people acceptable to Qianjiang. The peasants were furious, organized a petition, and sent Yao as a representative of Dongtan to Beijing to lodge a complaint with the State Bureau for Letters and Calls (Petition Bureau) of the National People's Congress.

Back in Dongtan, Yao and Yan organized information evenings for the peasants. There the villagers got crash courses in law and taxes. Many peasants' eyes must have been opened at that time. Yan tells journalists from Hong Kong that these meetings were filled with heated discussions and excitement. In Dongtan, militancy had reached a boiling point. "It was a fight to the finish," he says later. "*They* had cars and mobile phones; *we* had the law."

But the peasants had another weapon, a weapon from a fast-changing China: They called in the press. The *Hubei Daily News* stopped by, as did the national news service of China and finally the influential *Southern Weekend*. The story was picked up by the party administration in Beijing. Yao and Yan were gaining support.

The result was a resounding victory for Dongtan—even though it was short-lived. In April 2001, under pressure from Beijing and the provincial administration, elections were held again in the village. And this time the elections were free, as the progressive party leader had meant them to be. The winner was Zeng Xiangjun, the man who had asked questions about tuition. He became the new village head of Dongtan.

But the problems were not yet over. The township administration of Qianjiang still did not admit defeat. Even the hand of Beijing, admonishing words from the province, and reprimands from the district administration could not control the township. The administration refused to take action against an uncooperative treasurer of Dongtan who flatly refused to hand over the village stamp, which was necessary for all official actions, to the just-elected Zeng.

It turned out that the treasurer had in the past paid a considerable sum for the exclusive right to use this stamp (according to the villagers, so that he could practice unlimited fraud with it), and he wanted that money back.

Moreover, the township also refused to release the frozen village bank account. The brand-new committee could not get to its money.

More detective work showed that the previous village administration had plundered the village funds systematically. The former party secretary had appropriated considerable amounts of public funds to finance his daughter's private education. It turned out that over a period of three years more than $12,000 of public funds, taxes, and subsidies had been embezzled.

When the outcome of this investigation became known, the villagers refused to pay taxes any longer. This meant, of course, that they couldn't get anything done. After all, without money, there were no services. The township took no responsibility, condemned the peasants' behavior, and criticized the supposed lack of qualities of the elected village head, Zeng. But he was not intimidated. "I can't do anything without money," he said. Therefore, he lodged another complaint with the township.

The famous experiments with democracy have brought little good to Dongtan.

Guihong (rear, right) and his family among the plastic greenhouses that he brought along himself. For the occasion, every member of the family has dug up his or her cleanest and nicest clothing from someplace at the bottom of a bag or carryall. Only Guihong doesn't participate. "Let them see what I look like, I'm not ashamed," he says.

Always a Peasant

Substitute Sowers
(Zhejiang, Yiwu, Xiazucun)

The workers in sock factory "number two" couldn't believe their ears. Li Guihong had lived and worked in Shanghai for four years; he had successfully made the transition from peasant to factory worker; and after years of keeping his nose to the grindstone, he had a reasonably stable income. He had no reason to complain, and yet he wanted out.

Guihong had suddenly lost interest. He had not been able to stand factory life for some time. He wanted his freedom back. That was why he did something that no one understood: He wanted to become a farmer again.

"They thought I was out of my mind," says Guihong. "You don't come to the city to become a farmer, do you?" they had said. They were right, of course. The peasants had left their fields en masse because they were fed up with the uncertain existence on the land and because the prosperity in the cities enticed them. Going back to one's native soil to take up farming again was tantamount to capitulation.

But Guihong had another plan. He wanted to plow fields, but not his own. He wanted to work the land of rich peasants on the east coast. Those peasants were so busy doing other work that they didn't get to their own fields.

Peasant farmers like him were more than welcome there. And the work paid well.

"I'm a good farmer," says Guihong. "I know more about working the land than anything else." And even more important, "You're free on the land." He detests the factory. "When you report to the factory for the first time, you think, *This isn't so bad*. Promises are made: You get your pay at the end of the month; you can quit whenever you want. But after the first month's work the truth comes out: You get nothing! All of a sudden it's clear that you get paid at the end of a full year's work. 'Cash problems,' say the factory managers. But we know better."

To protest or to call the police is useless and even risky. "They seize your papers—as if you yourself are being seized. You've become their property. And that changes only if you stay for a long time; then you get back some security and money. That's why most workers keep quiet."

After four years in the factory, Guihong finally managed to save some money—approximately 2,000 yuan ($248) in his last year. He had done his work—changing and attaching spools of polyester thread—to the satisfaction of his boss, who had even promised him a promotion. Hence the surprise of his colleagues when he announced his plans. There were enough new employees who would love to trade places with Guihong.

"Factory work is really for young people," says Guihong. He is twenty-nine and apparently doesn't see himself as young. "When you're young and single, there's no problem. But if you're married and you have a child, then it becomes difficult. Factories don't take families into account. You can't house them anywhere and have to leave them behind at home, and you have to be able to stand that."

When the news of Guihong's planned departure from Shanghai reached his native village in Anhui, his wife, Xiao Siyuan, cursed and swore. It so happened that things were not going well at home in Zanggoucun. It had not rained for

The Lis harvest everything by hand. One motion of the arm suffices to strip bare a whole branch. What remains behind is a fistful of beans.

a long time, and the soil was as arid as ever. She was not looking forward to a demoralized husband without income.

But more important, what in heaven's name was Guihong going to do in Zanggoucun, the village he had left behind four years earlier with great plans? As if his life here had been so much better! Hadn't he constantly complained in Zanggoucun? About the disappointing harvests, the minimal earnings, the corrupt civil servants, and the lack of prospects and adventure.

Siyuan still remembers it well. During the weeks before Guihong's return, she had been very agitated. When he finally arrived, she was furious. Only then did he tell her his plan. He wanted to move the whole farm to arable land somewhere in one of the prosperous provinces near the coast. "Have you taken leave of your senses?" she had snapped. But Guihong didn't budge an inch. He was determined and immediately started collecting and tying up the agricultural plastic and the bamboo stays that he needed for his greenhouses.

In the months that followed, more and more family members started to join in Guihong's plans—his older brother, three sisters-in-law, and a cousin. They didn't think his plan was totally crazy. The persuasive powers of the three sisters-in-law had been needed to bring Guihong's wife around.

Together they then chose a destination. It was, in fact, an obvious one. Through other villagers, they knew that in the neighboring coastal province Zhejiang, south of Shanghai, plenty of land was available. The peasants there had been entrepreneurs for so long (starting in the early 1980s, right after the Communist Party had given its blessing), that many of them had neglected working the land. That created a problem, because it was forbidden to let the land lie fallow. And using the land for other purposes was not feasible. Increasingly, peasants from poor provinces like Anhui offered a solution to this problem, and the Lis had become aware of this.

It took them weeks to gather everything that needed to be moved. The move to Zhejiang was not forever, but an undertaking of this size was much more complicated than when peasants left for the city to look for work. Then a bag with clothes, a bedroll, and possibly a washtub were sufficient. But this time materials for greenhouses, plows, sowing seed, sacks of fertilizer, and all the household goods had to go. The Lis took with them everything they thought would be more expensive in Zhejiang.

The move took place by public transportation. "The whole roof of the bus was full to overflowing," Guihong recounts. He still gets tired when he thinks of it: how they had dragged all their things to the paved road; how they waited forever in the rain before finding a bus driver prepared, for a payment of course, to transport half a farm on his roof: how, finally, after a nauseating, bumpy, fifteen-hour ride, they were dropped in Futian.

But all their trouble had not been in vain. Futian was precisely as their fellow villagers had predicted. There was plenty of land, and the soil was good, much more fertile than in Anhui. Soil lay fallow everywhere, and the Lis could

Turning melons is important work. "Otherwise they'll rot," says Guihong. Bad ones are immediately thrown from the field. Guihong is not dissatisfied. He'll have a good harvest this year.

get to work right away. They cobbled together more than 2.5 acres from peasant entrepreneurs who had stopped sowing and harvesting. The Lis had never worked that much land; in Anhui they had plowed a little more than a quarter of an acre per person. But they managed quite well. In no time their vegetable production was thriving.

Shortly afterward, the district administration of Futian announced that the land would be claimed back by the government within a year. That was the way things went at the time. Because of its increasing population, Futian too was expanding rapidly and, as everywhere else in Zhejiang and along the Chinese coast, the district was designating more and more agricultural land as industrial zones.

The Lis were shocked but could do nothing. "The government decides, the land is theirs," Guihong says, resigned. Yet it was not a disaster for the Lis. "We were given a lot of time," and that mitigated the circumstances. While all of them had dreaded a new move so soon after the previous one, upon inquiry they found out that not far from Futian, in Yiwu, the soil was even more fertile.

BENT BAMBOO

In Xiazucun, a village a stone's throw from Yiwu, it has been raining all day. The noise of the water beating down sounds like raindrops on an umbrella; the Lis' "new" accommodation has a plastic roof—a greenhouse of bamboo arches and transparent agricultural plastic has been converted into a sleeping

The boys play and horse around and for the rest of the day do nothing. They can't go to school, and Guihong says they don't have to work.

and eating area. On the outside, a covering of reeds has been attached against the wind and cold, but it is not very effective.

It is the middle of the day, and Guihong, his wife, and his two sisters are playing mah-jongg, for money. They let the heavy stones glide deftly through their fingers, throw them down with sure hands, and mix them up again with large, stirring arm motions after each game. It produces a pleasant, familiar sound.

The Lis don't let themselves be rushed by anything or anyone. When it rains, they stay inside. "I work only when it's dry; I'm my own boss. When I want to rest, I do it." That, says Guihong, is the great advantage of being a peasant. "In the factory you have no freedom, you do overtime, and you never have time off. The only possible advantage is that you hardly have any responsibilities. You don't have to invest anything, and when it rains you keep on earning. Of course that's different on the land."

Guihong sees the factory as an alternative for difficult times. If the harvest is bad, they can always go to work on the assembly line. But that hasn't been necessary as yet. He earns enough, and not a day goes by without him realizing that his decision to leave Shanghai was the right one. "Every so often I still long for Shanghai—those beautiful streets and buildings. But it's hard to become part of all that. The opportunities for earning a lot of money are few and far between for a simple peasant."

Guihong feels more like himself as a farming peasant. "The peasants here don't know how to grow vegetables. It's warm here, the plants rot more quickly, and you have to use the right amount of pesticides. They harvest rice twice a year, no more." The Lis fill that gap by growing hot peppers, bell peppers, tomatoes, zucchinis, beans, melons, cucumbers, and cauliflower. "Many different products create stability," says Guihong wisely. He saw that on television, and it's a strategy that has done him no harm. He predicts that he'll earn about 10,500 yuan ($1,300) this year, much more than in the factory and considerably more than at home.

In Xiazucun, the Lis' lease for 2,100 yuan ($260) a total of twenty *mu* (3.25 acres) of strung-together patches of land from several villagers who gave up farming years ago. "We are at the upper limit of what we can do," says Guihong. "Much more land and we won't be able to keep up with the weeds." The Lis still weed by hand because their existence is too precarious to invest in machines. For instance, there is no question of a contract with the village administration ("We were willing, but they refused"), and they don't know at all how long they will be allowed to work the land. In addition, building on the land is not allowed; the plastic tent where they live is tolerated, but they have no electricity.

"The villagers aren't really friendly," says Guihong. The Lis are noticed when they draw water from the well or when the villagers buy vegetables from them at the side of the road, but that's about all the contact there is. "At home the people are more friendly than here. The people are poor, but they respect one another." Guihong is irritated by the arrogance and the lack of understanding for his family's living and working situation. "I don't really know all the rules. Sometimes we are fined for things we don't understand. Recently they cut off our drainage system, a punitive measure, but no one explained why."

Guihong thinks that's very unfair, especially because the prosperous villagers from Xiazucun, just as in the rest of Zhejiang, "flourish on the backs of poor peasants like me. Migrant workers populate the factories and construction pits. We produce the food that fills the bellies in the city. Without us, they're finished."

WHITE CITADELS

Nowhere are the peasants of China as rich as in the prosperous coastal area between Shanghai and Hong Kong. The villages of Zhejiang have an urban aura and from afar they look like white citadels in an oasis of green. The white-tiled façades of the densely massed houses tower high above the agricultural land. The taller the houses, the greater the wealth. Xiazucun has so many tall houses that it barely passes for a village in Chinese eyes.

The largest and flashiest house is that of the party secretary. It stands at the edge of the village, right on the main village street. The characteristic bathroom tiles are set in big arches around the Romanesque windows, and all the fences and railings in front of the windows, at the outside gate, and at the main gate are made of the same chrome pipes that are used at many Chinese airports. This peasant citadel has the appearance of an airport. No attempt is made here to hide wealth; everyone is welcome to the information: The party secretary is rich. He earned it honestly with his own calendar factory, the villagers say.

Most villagers have found work in Yiwu. This city was the first place in China where the wholesale trade in consumer articles was started. As early as 1982, illegal trade was taking place in Yiwu, which at the time was still a small, ugly provincial town. The planned economy did not permit this, but the peasants of Yiwu paid no attention. Far away from the center of power in Beijing, Yiwu was determined to grow, and two years later the city grew so convincingly that the district administration received official permission to continue the experiment. Attracted by the convincing success stories, more and more peasants from the surrounding area took the plunge as entrepreneurs.

Meanwhile, Yiwu provides all of China with products. From all parts of the country traders flock to Yiwu, and many foreigners—Russians, Pakistanis, Indians, and Afghans—have also found their way to the city in Zhejiang. More than fifty-three thousand market booths and 160,000 merchants supply the needs of two hundred thousand visitors daily.

Everywhere in Yiwu, high-rises with plate-glass façades are springing up—there is no economic success in China without glittering high-rise complexes. And behind these façades is a man's world of buyers and sellers, where hotels, restaurants, and prostitutes cater to the needs of a constant stream of businesspeople. Conversations on the street are about money, and street children earn their money with songs about rich entrepreneurs who can maintain more than one woman: *Laopo yue duo, yue kuai huo. Laoban ting wo shuo, zhu ni zhaodao ba ge laopo!* (The more women the quicker the satisfaction. Listen to me, boss, I wish you eight women!)

In Xiazucun only crazy people and the elderly who live alone still depend on the land, according to the general public. Peasants with even an ounce of mercantile spirit simply buy their rice and vegetables at the market because they are busy with their trade in Yiwu. Wu Weiping is one of these, an ex-peasant. He is thirty-nine and has left his peasant existence for good. For five hundred years the Wus from Xiazucun had plowed, sowed, and harvested here, until the youngest descendant gave it up. Full-time entrepreneurship—Weiping started a trade in temple copper (candlesticks, gongs, clocks, little bells, and censers)—took all his time.

He still spends every day in the immense market hall where all the peasant entrepreneurs from Yiwu and its surroundings try to sell huge amounts of merchandise for rock-bottom prices. Most of the smaller entrepreneurs, like Weiping, sit, slouch, or sleep there all day behind their small iron stalls, while waiting for the one client who will perhaps buy most of the lot. For Weiping it's not about a single candlestick or bell. "My smallest bell [the size of a pea] costs half a fen [$0.0007]. That's not how you get rich. It only gets interesting when you sell a whole lot of them, fifty thousand bells, for instance. I do that regularly."

Meanwhile, the seven *mu* (1.16 acres) of land that the Wus, a family of thirteen, controlled, have been lying fallow. They were forbidden to lease the land out to other peasants from the village. This has to do with a 1985 regulation, when the land was allotted to the peasants for fifty years, and no one except for the village committee could make independent decisions about this. Moreover, there was a lottery to decide which families could work where. Weiping

Work in the market hall is not tiring. There is very little demand for Weiping's temple copper. The few people who stop at his stall can choose among many vendors. That's what makes things so difficult according to Weiping. He and his wife (holding child at left) wait day in day out for a buyer who will buy up their stall.

explains that this happens every thirty years. In this way no one can take possession of the best piece of land around the village for a long time.

Ultimately the village administration, following the example of other prosperous villages in the region, decided to approve leasing the peasants' land to peasant farmers from outside the area. In this way the land continued to be worked and the food production was kept at the same level without migrant workers being able to claim right of ownership. "Formerly agricultural land was a stable factor in everyone's existence. But no longer," says Weiping. "Anytime the government wants to, it can claim back the land, especially if the peasants who were supposed to till it have other income." This means that those fifty years are not a guarantee. "Even four days are no guarantee," says Weiping. Therefore, he suspects that it won't be long before all of Xiazucun's agricultural land will disappear—swallowed by houses and office buildings. "I give it five years."

Until that time, migrant peasants will farm the land.

There is a coming and going of peasants from the poorer neighboring provinces. "Most of them don't stay much longer than a year." Weiping scratches his head, trying to remember the name of the tenants who are currently working the land belonging to his own family. "I barely know these people," says Weiping apologetically. But after thinking a while he remembers the name: the Lis from Anhui.

A FALLING-OUT

Underneath the taut tent cloth in Guihong's tamped-down field there is an infernal racket. If you didn't know better, it sounds almost like a life-and-death struggle. Loud women's voices rise above men's shouting. The tone is aggressive, but luckily there is laughter as well. Guihong assures me later that nothing is wrong—it's "just" bargaining.

It is the end of the week and a middleman has dropped in. "But didn't we help you, too?" one of Guihong's sisters-in-law shouts at him. She has a voice like a foghorn, shakes her head indignantly, and paces back and forth angrily in the tent. She doesn't stay angry very long; she means it, but much of the loud outrage is playacting.

Then Guihong's wife takes over. She's also quite good at it. "Ten yuan more or less, what do you care, you make money hand over fist, but we live only one day on it. You have it easy. You're trying to play a nasty trick on us!" Accusingly she shakes a finger at the middleman's face.

He sniggers. He reminds the Lis that he too used to be a peasant and therefore can readily understand that they don't have it easy. But he really can't give them what they are asking. "I have to earn something myself!" he exclaims indignantly. "You're earning plenty," Guihong counters. And what's more, the Lis helped him in the past when, because of a wrong estimate, he ended up with excess vegetables. They had simply bought the lot from him. "It's your turn to help us!"

The whole family gets involved. There is renewed shouting and laughing. But then it's suddenly over. All at once the middleman and the Lis cave in and agree to a price that pleases everyone.

When the middleman has finally left, Guihong sighs with exhaustion. "That's exactly why some people prefer to take their products to market themselves. To avoid dealing with this kind of person."

Guihong's oldest brother is one of these people who avoids the middleman. His name is Huaihong, he is thirty-three, and he has a mustache just like his brother. But he looks more serious. "The price in the city is higher," he says. Huaihong earns good money from his vegetables. He detests merchants. "I prefer doing it myself." But to do it himself he does have to get up at an ungodly hour every day, as early as two in the morning. "I bicycle with a full load for two hours to get there. Most restaurants buy their produce between three and five in the morning."

Once in a while he doesn't feel like getting up, especially when it rains, but the extra income makes it worthwhile. "I have two boys, one is twelve and the other is eleven. That's expensive. When the second one was born, I was fined 700 yuan [$86]! Pretty soon they'll finish school, and then they'll get married. I'm saving for a house for each of them. That will cost 70,000 yuan [$8,680]. I'll have that in six years."

Huaihong seems more decisive and energetic than his brother. He thinks so, too. "I earn more, but I also work harder." That is why, he explains, the brothers keep their businesses strictly separated. "In that way we have no conflicts." Were there any? "Oh, I don't want to be a bother to him," he says. But then he adds, "His wife and mine don't care for each other. It's better this way."

Therefore, when Huaihong and his wife harvest their produce on a parcel

Huaihong working in front of his rental home. The only reason he can afford that house is because he works much harder than his brother Guihong. "I do nothing but work," he says while tying together the long beans in order to sell them in the local market.

that borders Guihong's, the rest of the family looks the other way. The brothers don't speak to each other. Huaihong and his wife have rented a place in Xiazucun.

"It costs me 80 yuan per month," he says about the old house on a dead-end alley in the center of the village. It has no tiled façade or other luxury. The two-room apartment is actually nothing more than a double cement space that serves primarily as storage space for the harvest. On the wall is a poster with pictures of 100 yuan bills, the largest banknote in China. "That brings good luck," says Huaihong's wife.

"I live here because I don't sleep much. It's warm in Guihong's tent, and it's infested with mosquitoes. I sleep better here," Huaihong lies. Not a disparaging word about his brother.

Just like Guihong, Huaihong has traded factory work for life on the land. "For several years I made brooms in Anhui. I earned a lot of money doing that. Then I started a trade in ice blocks with a couple of friends in Shanghai." Huaihong sold the 260-pound ice blocks to market companies and fishmongers. "Heavy work that was poorly paid," he says. Ultimately that was the reason he left the city and followed his brother to Futian and Yiwu. "I earn more quickly here," he says.

But his life is not any easier. When Huaihong has any leftover produce after he harvests his vegetables, he sells the rest in a village near Xiazucun. He does this illegally, for the village allows trade only in the designated village market hall. "But for that you need a permit, and they issue them for only a year." That's too expensive for Huaihong.

Several times a week he stands at the entrance of the street leading to the market, nervously looking around. This practice is not without danger. On the day that I watch him hawking his bundles of black-eyed peas from his delivery bicycle, he almost gets beaten by a uniformed supervisor of the market hall.

Huaihong, who has no license, steals customers from others who do have one, and that is not tolerated. The supervisor pulls his belt from his trousers and threatens to give him a beating. So Huaihong takes off in the middle of a transaction and goes back to business a little farther away. He is able to laugh about it, but his customers chasing after him for their change don't think it's funny.

"Women are a blessing and a curse," says Guihong in his wife's presence. "They provide stability, but if they start quarreling, then they do a lot of harm." He doesn't want to say anything about the family feud, but the break with his brother obviously bothers him. "Together we were stronger."

When it is windy and rainy, the Lis are sometimes afraid. The plastic greenhouse that serves as living room and bedroom is sturdy, says Guihong, but it can easily spring a leak. When it actually does leak, the Lis simply push their beds to the side.

He doesn't know what the future of vegetable growing in Xiazucun will be, especially now that his wife threatens to return to Anhui. She is pregnant and will deliver at home because the hospitals in Zhejiang are too expensive. Besides, she wants to go with Mengran, their seven-year-old daughter, who has to go to school and, again to reduce expenses, is better off in Zanggoucun. "We'll manage," says Guihong during his evening meal. He doesn't sound convinced.

When night falls, it is still raining. It is pitch-black outside and only the white neon light from a huge textile factory across from the Lis' field cuts a white stripe through the darkness. Inside, the deafening patter of the rain on the plastic roof continues. It leaks here and there, but no one cares. Guihong has lit a candle and lies in bed together with his wife and small child—it is a screened-off corner between dirty pillows and blankets on a wooden platform. He reads a little in the flickering light until his eyes close.

Mengran, who is still awake, blows out the candle stub.

证

Epilogue

Fear and the Peasant Migration

It isn't until you have lost something that you know what you are missing. That's about the way the city appreciates its peasant guests—not out of affection but because of inconvenience. When the peasant workers leave the city en masse—which they do once a year—a large part of public life is completely at a standstill.

When this happens, coal is no longer delivered, no one picks up the garbage in the narrow alleys, door-to-door deliveries of milk, vegetables, and beer are halted, families are without a babysitter for their child, restaurants close their doors temporarily, there are no steaming breakfast stalls on the streets, no one receives newspapers at home, all construction projects are interrupted, and factories close temporarily.

Without the peasants, the city functions at half power. It certainly is inefficient. But no city dweller is willing to take over the underpaid, unpleasant, and dirty jobs of the migrant peasants, not even for a short while. As a result, nothing at all happens for a short time in many service sectors when the migrants are away, around Chinese New Year in January or February and around harvest time in September.

But this situation brings an incidental benefit that some city dwellers enjoy:

the relative quiet that descends on the cities. Rushing around leads to nothing during that time. Here and there, even though it's in out-of-the-way alleys, old-fashioned silence even breaks through, but it never prevails.

The New Year announces itself with a thunderous bang. The returned migrants rush back into the city like a herd of buffalo that makes the ground shake for miles before reaching their destination. They return in packed trains or buses and, after their arrival, on getting out, almost flatten one another against the closely placed crush barriers. They are well fed and full of new energy, which has already sustained a considerable dent after a sleepless trip back to the city.

The yearning in the city for the hardworking peasants disappears on their return like snow melting in the sun. The political and social apartheid of the peasants quickly takes on its usual shape once again, and sympathy for the migrants, if there ever was any, is out of the question.

Every year the enormous inconvenience caused by the yearly mega-move results in much discussion, and important party officials say that it really can't go on any longer. But as soon as the travel season has passed and the peasants have retaken their places in the city, the public discussion about the peasants is directed once again to their presence. For the peasants keep coming.

Everyone keeps hammering on the danger of the peasant invasion—especially the police. Criminality seems to be taking on alarming proportions. Investigation after investigation—ordered by the government—must show that these worries are appropriate.

And this is expressed in percentages, for the Chinese policy makers are crazy about those. In the port city of Tianjin, for example, the migrant workers seem to be responsible for 35 percent of all crimes; in Shenzhen it's 25 percent. At the present there seem to be ten times more holdups than there were ten years ago. In the past several years, the number of murders has supposedly risen by 40 percent. And in comparison to 1995, the year when the dangers of the growing migrant army were debated for the first time, the number of crimes has supposedly increased by half. All this is supposedly the consequence of the massive influx of migrant workers.

According to most Chinese criminologists, the origin of all this evil is jealousy. Jealousy thrives in a climate of growing inequality. "Poverty and materialism have become a big problem," says Xu Jian of China's Juvenile Crime Studies Association. "People are increasingly confronted with the affluence of others and become jealous. That happens to many migrant workers, who ask themselves more and more often: 'Why exactly are we so poor?' " It's a pertinent question, according to Xu. Some peasants become so frustrated by the injustice they experience that they become confirmed criminals.

In this connection the Zhang Jun affair is often mentioned in China. At the end of the 1990s Zhang Jun was known as "China's number one enemy of the people"—and with reason. Zhang was a man for whom violence was as normal as stubbing out a cigarette. He made legendary criminals like Al Capone and Bonnie and Clyde pale into ordinary shoplifters with behavior problems. Zhang murdered to his heart's content. He preferred to pull the trigger when the barrel of his pistol was against the temple of his victim. And he did that as many as twenty-seven times before he was arrested in September 2000, to everyone's relief.

After the outcome of this affair, the migrant workers saw that the stigma that existed against them had only been strengthened. Zhang Jun was not an ordinary Chinese; he was a drifting unemployed migrant worker from the countryside. His violent wanderings confirmed many city dwellers' greatest fear: the criminal drive of the impoverished peasant class. The city was warned once again: In the long run, many more poor peasants would come and teach the rich city dwellers a lesson.

The prominent Chinese economist Hu Angang can't believe his ears. Hu, who is respected in China and does not avoid controversy, speaks about a great prejudice against peasants. According to him, the so-called migrant criminality does not exist, and he totally rejects the idea of a possible revolt. However, he does believe that a general sense of values is fading and that criminality has increased. But he feels that this is the consequence of the market economic changes that are influencing China. Hu says that the growing gap between poor and rich incites the underprivileged at all levels of the population to objectionable behavior. "Seeing migrant workers as potential criminals is nothing but discrimination." These are daring notions for a Chinese scholar.

But there are also Chinese economists who point to unreasonable employers as the cause of the problem. They state that it is the very misconduct of managers and bosses that incites violence. In 2005 a man was condemned to death after he murdered a factory manager and three of his colleagues because they had systematically refused to pay him the earnings to which he was entitled. The factory had owed him 5,000 yuan. The Chinese politicians were so alarmed by the affair concerning this Wang Binyu that Prime Minister Wen Jiabao called for solving the question of structural wage arrears within three years.

This criticism of migrant workers in China does not differ very much from that in the West. There, too, the public regularly lashes out at guest workers, who, according to some, are more of a pain than a pleasure. "The peasants are taking our jobs," say the people in the cities. But nothing is further from the truth. Just as in the West, most Chinese city dwellers turn up their noses at the work that is being done by the migrants.

This also explains why it is so much easier for migrants to find work than for well-educated Chinese. In the spring of 2002, the *Shenzhen Economic Daily* reported with some fanfare that unemployment among recent college graduates was much higher than among migrant workers. In Shenzhen 17 percent of the college graduates were unemployed, 12 percent more than in the previous year. Conversely, there was no unemployment at all among the not particularly choosy migrants.

The growing fear of being overrun by the peasants has increased as the economic climate in the cities has deteriorated. During the 1990s countless people lost their jobs. And the permanent closing or reorganization of money-losing government enterprises that took place on a large scale during the last few years of the twentieth century caused millions of city dwellers to lose their jobs. It appears that between 1998 and 2002, 23 million people lost their jobs just in the industrial sector.

Officially it is said that there is 5.6 percent unemployment in China, but no one knows for sure. What is certain is that one factory after the other has closed its doors and that this trend has not stopped yet, not even after China's admittance to the World Trade Organization.

The Chinese authorities have reacted frantically and inconsistently to this situation. Peasants are both encouraged to come to the cities and discouraged from doing so. A huge number of regulations have been devised by the police to counter the stream of migrants, and all big cities now have a policy of determent, instituted on orders of the Ministry of Labor, which has no better solutions and champions the employment situation of the city dwellers.

The policy of banning migrants from occupations exists in many cities and is a good example of this deterrent policy. Several cities employ such a policy, but until 2005 Beijing was the absolute leader. In the past ten years it has decided to expand the number of occupations forbidden for peasants from forty to more than one hundred. Peasants were not allowed to work in hotels, have jobs in the tourist industry, do bookkeeping, or work in private enterprises.

In March of 2005, the Beijing People's Congress concluded that these regulations had turned out to be unworkable. Because of enormous demand, the peasants were badly needed in Beijing, and thus the job limitations were abolished from one day to the next.

But other cities don't want to do this for the time being. The fact that these job limitations run completely counter to the cities' economic interests is a secondary consideration that those city administrations don't take into account or that they are undecided about at the very least.

Since a new party administration took office in 2003 under the leadership of Hu Jintao, the government seems slightly more sensitive to this problem and has called the cities to account. "We have to try harder to help the peasants in finding work in the city and to end these discriminating regulations and levies that are imposed on the migrant workers," said President Hu Jintao in December 2003. The concept that peasants contribute to progress has finally gotten across to the party leadership. To acknowledge this, the party decided at the end of 2005 to recognize the migrants in their own special way. The recognition happened according to good Communist custom by honoring six "outstanding" migrant workers in the Great Hall of the People in Beijing. The six were thanked for their "great contribution" to Chinese prosperity and were declared "model workers."

There has been much speculation about the worth of Chinese migrant workers, but no one can describe in exact numbers how indispensable they actually are. Only a few cities have figured it out, and the conclusion is not surprising: The peasants make an incredibly large contribution to the economies of large cities.

For instance, the city administration of the previously mentioned port city of Tianjin calculated in 2000 that the 1.1 million migrant workers (one-tenth of the total number of inhabitants) who worked in the city contributed $1.2 billion in income. In addition, they yearly spent $420 million of their income, just in Tianjin.

In 2002 the Chinese government determined that, assuming a migrant population of 70 million peasants, the migrants had pumped close to $16 billion into the Chinese hinterland in the previous few years, money that they had earned in the cities and had sent home. Labor economist Cai Fang even believes that migrants who in 2000 had worked in the cities for more than six months sent an average of $540 home, as a result of which those who stayed home received as much as $36.6 billon. This is closer to the calculations of Wang Xiaolu of the National Economic Research Bureau. He thinks that the peasants from the large cities sent home $55 billion in 2003, or 3.9 percent of the national income—an enormous economic stimulus.

All things considered, the anti-peasant regulations are therefore rather shortsighted and the call for a more just treatment of peasants is becoming ever louder. But what is usually at issue is fear instead of compassion. In a wider context, Chinese politicians have often pointed to the danger of the existing inequality in China. It has by now become a cliché, but the Communist Party owes its power to a great extent to the peasants, while the peasants have in fact become second-rank citizens. The party is well aware of this.

Chinese scholars have delved in more detail into the problem of apartheid in society. Many studies have been done into the consequences of a de facto segregated form of education that makes peasant children realize at an early age that they live in a class society where they and their parents are always the losers.

Lu Jufu, member of an advisory panel of the Communist Party and affiliated with the University of Xiamen in south China, argues that the children of migrant workers will have other expectations than their parents had. "What do the children think, who, unlike their parents, have lived all their school years on the periphery of society? They feel unjustly treated, and that can provoke a lot of hostility in the future."

Nowhere in Asia are income inequalities as lopsided as in China. According to a few people, that is so because the peasants don't assert themselves sufficiently. How is it, for example, that China has an organization for everything—for women, students, journalists, writers, and Taoists—but not for the peasants, the largest population group in the land?

In September 2003, China's only union, the All China Federation of Trade Unions, permitted "established" migrant peasants to become members. According to the union, 6 million migrants joined in 2006. But most peasants feel unprotected. They prefer to turn to the so-called *tongxianghui*, or village associations, which have no influence but with which they feel at home.

For obvious reasons, Beijing does not permit the formation of such a potentially powerful group—except for a few experiments in places like Yiwu and Rui'an (both in Zhejiang Province) and Shanghai (where 1 million migrants, one-fourth of the city's total migrant population, are now members of a union). But is it logical that businessmen are nowadays permitted to become members of the Communist Party while peasants are not even allowed to start their own organization? There isn't a peasant who says anything about it.

Again it's the scholars, not the peasants, who dare to comment on this in public. According to Dang Guoying of the Chinese Academy for Social Sciences, it is only with the help of *nonghui*, or peasant organizations, that peasant dissatisfaction can be prevented. "Unorganized dissatisfaction on the land is the basis for a peasant revolution," he says. As far as he is concerned, a peasant organization that can lobby the government is needed to curb massive dissatisfaction.

Practically every problem in China is a problem of massiveness. The time when overpopulation was a good thing is long gone; it gave up the ghost in the mid-1970s on the last great battlefield of China's history, at the end of the Cultural Revolution. Since then massiveness has chiefly become a problem.

One of the most important consequences of overpopulation is fear: the leaders' fear of letting go and giving the people more freedom, and the individual's fear of rising above the mass and sticking out his neck. Overpopulation and fear have China in a stranglehold.

Wen Tiejun, a former researcher at the Ministry of Agriculture, believes that China, with its population of 1.3 billion, needs only 100 million real farmers—provided that agriculture becomes modernized, small-scale farms disappear, and China does not hesitate to import grain. What that really means is a nightmare for every administrator. Because 100 million working farmers means 400 million to 500 million superfluous peasants who have to find employment elsewhere.

The fact is that conditions are bad in the countryside. Approximately 120 million peasants live below subsistence level. Rural industry, until recently an important employer, is in crisis. At the peak of the development of rural factories, in 1996, approximately 135 million peasants were employed, but in a few years' time their share decreased by almost 10 million jobs. And no one believes that this reduction will stop. Work is being done more and more efficiently in the cities, and the small peasant companies, cement factories, tile makers, glassblowers, plastic casters, electronic parts makers, porcelain producers, motorbike factories, and similar small industries can't compete with their city counterparts.

But the problem is not that simple. The prices of agricultural products have dropped continually, while raw materials such as sowing seed, fertilizer, and pesticides have become much more expensive. The European Union has calculated that since China's entry into the World Trade Organization in 2001, the production of grain, soybeans, and corn has decreased substantially because import tariffs for agricultural products have decreased by half. The result is that at least 13 million peasant farmers have lost income and threaten to abandon their farms completely. The peasant invasion of the cities is not anywhere near finished. More and more politicians think that this invasion is necessary to offer the peasants prospects. But they disagree about the way this must happen. Here is the big conflict: To guarantee stability on the land, more peasants must go to the city, but massive urbanization happens at the expense of stability in the city.

Yet this concept, the depopulation of China's countryside, is basically revolutionary. Opinions on this topic vary: "The number of peasants must be decreased radically; only then can farmers' incomes grow. Without urbanization, the peasant class can never develop," says Chen Xiwen, deputy director of the special research center of the State Council, the Chinese cabinet.

"China has too little agricultural land and too many people who have to live from it. The people have to go, for we can't conjure up agricultural land," says the previously mentioned Wen Tiejun of the Ministry of Agriculture.

"Cheap labor will be China's trump card until well into the twenty-first century. Where can it be found? On the land. Let the peasants come. The peasants are China's future," says Cai Fang of the Population Institute of the Chinese Academy for Social Sciences.

And finally a report from China Capital Corporation, a Chinese think tank, says, "China can never modernize its economy without a drastic adjustment of the population structure of the country." It's Communist blasphemy—but it is being said.

Politicians and scholars feel that the peasants must keep coming, and in this opinion they are diametrically opposed to the large cities' administrations that want to get rid of the peasants. For instance, the party's tenth five-year plan (2001–2005) did not take into account the objections of the cities. It made urbanization a priority and stated that another 85 million peasants had to move to the city within the period of the plan.

Within six years, 40 percent of the Chinese population will have to live in a city. According to official numbers, a little more than one-third of China is urbanized (compared to 70 percent in the developed world), as much as the urbanization in Great Britain around 1850. Critical demographers think the current urbanization rate is only 18 percent (200 million urbanized Chinese).

In 2001 Beijing made family registration (*hukouzhidu*) easier in order to speed up urbanization. Since that liberalization, peasants have been permitted to move to any city within their home province. And when those migrants can prove that they have had a stable income there for two consecutive years, they are entitled to a residence permit for that provincial city. Discrimination in awarding jobs on the basis of *hukou* is forbidden by law. In this way the Chinese government hopes to close the wide income gap between the peasants and the city dwellers more quickly.

But on this point opinions are divided as well. A small minority of politicians and scholars resists the government's intention to create new provincial cities of two hundred thousand inhabitants. According to the Ministry of Civilian Affairs, twenty of these cities will be needed yearly over a period of twenty years, and in this way the constant stream to the very largest and most overpopulated cities can be slowed.

The critics believe that such a small-scale policy (by Chinese standards) costs too much money and will ultimately come at the expense of scarce agricultural land. That last point in particular has been discussed a lot. Ultimately so little suitable agricultural land would remain in the fertile areas of China that the country will be unable to provide for its ever-increasing need for food.

No matter how incredible it may sound, satellite photos have shown that

China has in recent years lost approximately 3.7 million acres of agricultural land to urbanization and industrialization. A special law, the Land Use Law, which is supposed to prevent loss of land, has helped very little until now.

Fan Gang, the director of the independent National Economic Research Institute in Beijing and one of the most outspoken critics of the Chinese population policy, likes radical measures. What China needs, he says, are megacities of at least 2 million inhabitants, cities that must be created from already existing cities—not the building of new cities. "Today's cities can become much larger," he says. "In the next fifteen years we will need between fifty and one hundred of these cities." Fan finds that projection "reasonable" and feasible. According to Fan, the problems that are guaranteed to result—heavy traffic, environmental deterioration, and urban decay—can all be tolerated because "the pain is only temporary" and "is completely outweighed by the prevention of explosive inequality" that exists in China—bold language that is seldom heard in China.

Urbanization is needed because the peasant invasion is inevitable. For most city dwellers, this is not a pleasant prospect. When China actually attempts to close the gap between rich and poor, the quality of life of the average city dweller will not improve for some time.

The city administration of Fuxin in the northeastern province of Liaoning is not waiting for disaster and is the first city in China that has encouraged its unemployed inhabitants to leave the city. With the motto "Seize your chance and become a farmer," three thousand former mine workers have found work in fifteen modern farms financed by the state. This is in complete accordance with Mao Zedong's revolutionary wish to let city dwellers work in the fields so that the city will learn from the countryside.

It is the world turned upside down. The "modern-style peasants" are no peasant migrants but "city migrants," city dwellers who become farmers. There is not a farmer in China who will understand that.

件

About the Author and the Photographers

Floris-Jan van Luyn studied history and Chinese in Groningen, Leiden, Taipei, and Beijing. He started his career in journalism as an assistant to Nicholas Kristof, the *New York Times* correspondent in Beijing. Subsequently he was an intern at the *Trouw* daily and on the editorial staff of *NRC Handelsblad*. In 1995, the Dutch national daily *NRC Handelsblad* sent him to Beijing, where he worked as a correspondent until 2001. In those six years, Van Luyn concentrated on meeting ordinary people, which resulted in his interest in migrant workers. From 2001 until 2004, Van Luyn was North American and Southeast Asian editor for that same newspaper. Subsequently he became an independent journalist and filmmaker. In the Netherlands he participates regularly as a guest speaker in panel discussions about China. At present he is working on a book about the Yangtze and Mississippi rivers and on a film about the historical little alley next to Tiananmen Square where he lived during his years as a correspondent. His first film, *Cyber Coolies*, about Chinese peasants without land who harvest virtual gold, was made in 2006. *A Floating City of Peasants* is his first book.

Zhao Tielin was born in the year that the People's Republic of China was established. He was originally an engineer, trained at the Aviation and Space

Travel Academy of Beijing, and specializing in automatic guidance systems of airplanes and rockets. In 1990 Zhao quit his job at the Mathematics Institute of Beijing. From that time on he has completely concentrated on photography. Self-taught and with a great talent for images, he developed an interest in the fringes of Chinese society at the outset. His moving series about street children, prostitutes, fishermen's families, and life on a garbage dump break new ground in China. With his photos, which very often treat controversial subjects, Zhao does not pull any punches. The Chinese media publish Zhao's work without going into detail about its source and content. In this way Zhao is tolerated in China and is applauded by many. The series of photos in this book was made over a period of seven years. Other work by Zhao was shown at the Photo Festival in Naarden (the Netherlands) in 2001. (Zhao Tielin's photographs appear on pages 100, 103, 104, 111, 135, and 216.)

The first time that **Vincent Mentzel** set foot on Chinese soil was in 1973. At that time he was staff photographer for *NRC Handelsblad* and part of the delegation of the then Dutch minister of economic affairs, Ruud Lubbers. The Cultural Revolution was still in full swing. At that time only official delegations and one or two journalists traveling with them were permitted to take a peek into the still-isolated country. In 1979 World Press Photo awarded first prize to Mentzel's series about Mongolia. In 1980 and 1981 he worked in Tibet and Xinjiang for the first time. His photos again won a World Press Photo prize. Mentzel is still a staff photographer at *NRC Handelsblad* and is also editor of the monthly magazine *M* published by that paper. (Vincent Mentzel's photographs appear on pages 30, 32, 37, 55, 57, 96, 98, 113, 114, 151, 152, 154, 156, 158, 161, 166, and 167.)

Liu Jingxing works at the Bureau for Environmental Protection in Beijing. Through that position he has come in contact with the garbage workers from Sichuan. He visits them almost weekly and has photographed them many times over a seven-year period. Liu is very sympathetic to his friends who handle garbage. He advises and assists them and enjoys his special friendship with the garbagemen from Sichuan, even though as a city dweller he would be their natural enemy. The photos in *A Floating City of Peasants* are the result of that friendship. Some of them were made especially for *A Floating City of Peasants*, while others came from Liu's unused and unpublished files. (Liu Jingxing's photographs appear on pages 58, 63, 64, 65, 67, 68, 74, and 79.)

Yang Yankang started his career as a machinist in a sock factory. In 1984 he left for Shenzhen, where he began work in the distribution department of a photo magazine. A year later he started making photos himself, and this soon led to his establishment of a photo studio. His first solo exhibitions were in Shenzhen, Guizhou, and Xi'an. In 1992 his work was part of a German exhibition about the Chinese countryside. Yang Yangkang has also exhibited work in Japan. Starting in 1996 he has shown photos of Chinese Catholics. The subject moved him so much that he has converted to Catholicism. As founder and owner of the Shenzhen Photo Bureau, he is currently very busy with commercial photography, which enables Yang Yankang to finance his probing reports elsewhere in China. His photos were made especially for *A Floating City of Peasants*. (Yang Yankang's photographs appear on pages 10, 13, 15, 27, 94, and 220.)

Li Nan started out as a painter and was trained at the art academy of Shandong. During his studies, which he completed in 1993, he worked for twelve years as textile designer in a textile factory. As a socially active student, he became involved with the propaganda department of an organization for the handicapped in Jinan. There he decided to become a full-time photographer. Before that time, in the 1980s, he occasionally made photo strips. That was before television, when these special strips enjoyed great popularity. Li Nan aims his lens primarily at the less privileged and at old injustices in society: the blind, orphans, and women with bound feet. "During the Cultural Revolution, my father was labeled a 'rightist' and therefore I had a difficult youth. I think that's why I have a weakness for vulnerable people." He won first prize in the art category of World Press Photo in 1996 because of this involvement. In subsequent years he has won many Chinese and foreign prizes, among them the first prize of FIAP, the French international organization for photography. The photos in this book were made especially for *A Floating City of Peasants*. (Li Nan's photographs appear on pages 139, 180, 183, 185, 186, 191, 194, and 196.)

Michael S. Cherney majored in Asian Studies at Binghamton University in New York. In 1989 he studied Chinese in Taipei, Taiwan, where he met Van Luyn. Two years later, both men studied at the Language Institute in Beijing. Since that time Cherney and Van Luyn have frequently collaborated for *NRC Handelsblad* and other publications. A passion for photography runs in Cherney's family. His maternal grandfather was Charles Hoff, the *New York Daily Telegraph* photographer who became known through his famous photo of the exploding Hindenburg in 1937. After his study of Chinese, photographer, artist, and calligrapher Cherney decided to follow in his grandfather's footsteps, and since 1997 he has frequently traveled and photographed in China. His artwork, partly based on his photos, can be found, among other places, in the permanent collections of the Metropolitan Museum of Art in New York, the Getty Research Institute in Los Angeles, and the Santa Barbara Museum of Art. His photos were made especially for *A Floating City of Peasants*. (Michael S. Cherney's photographs appear on pages 130, 142, 145, 146, and 150.)

反对撕毁
任何证件

The sentence "You can't just tear up someone's identity card" comes from the poem "Against All Organized Deception" by Yan Jun (1973). Critic, publicist, and artist, Yan is considered a prominent person in the underground music scene of Beijing. The poem "Against All Organized Deception" is a long and inflammatory pamphlet, written in 2000, that speaks out about everything that Yan encounters—including the tearing up of identity cards.

Migrant children playing with medical waste, Haikou

Acknowledgments

Chinese migrant workers are reticent about the things they divulge since they are always suspicious about the intentions of an unfamiliar interviewer. Perhaps that is why it is unusual to see books about Chinese migrants in which the migrants themselves speak.

In this book I did not focus my attention on the limited research that already exists. Instead, I wanted to base my information primarily on impressions gathered from the peasants themselves. *A Floating City of Peasants* would not have been written without the willingness of the hundreds of peasants who shared their stories. They overcame their fear and their reticence, and their remarks are the principal part of this book.

The stories from Ganbacun and Xiaogang (poverty), Dongtougan (corruption), and Peijiazhuang (justice) are based on some of my previously published reports in *NRC Handelsblad*.

Several people, but in particular one institution, have had a great influence on the creation of this book. That institution is *NRC Handelsblad*; the general editors and the international editors of that paper were responsible for my being able to live, travel, and write in China for six years.

My special thanks go to the bureau editor for Asia, Wim Brummelman, a passionate West Asia traveler who shares my enthusiasm for China and advised and assisted me during our daily morning discussions.

Many people have been involved behind the scenes in the creation of *A Floating City of Peasants*. My special thanks go to Zhao Tielin and Liu Jingxing. Throughout the project, both photographers have pointed out persons, places, and texts that I would not have noticed without their experience and their eyes and ears.

In almost all the villages and cities that I visited during this project I was assisted by helpful and well-informed people: in Shanghai, Zhou Junwei and Kathelijn Verstraete; in Yiwu, Frost Huang and Garrie van Pinxteren; in Haikou, Hu Yaling and Zhang Xiong; in Changsha, Huang Fang; and in Shenzhen, photographer Yang Yankang. Many thanks to all.

Much information would have been missing from the reports that I wrote during the time that I was a correspondent—and therefore from this book—without the help of Song Gang. He assisted me as a sounding board and a well-informed source during four of the six years when I was a correspondent. Later Lao Zhang took over that task. Their insights have been invaluable.

I am also very grateful to Graham Hutchings, a former China correspondent of the British paper the *Daily Telegraph*, who witnessed my first journalistic steps and who acted as my mentor and familiarized me with many issues in China. His help and friendship have been indispensable.

Many thanks also to Maghiel van Crevel, who brought the poem by Yan Jun to my attention.

For bringing about the English-language publication, I want to express my thanks to Caroline van Gelderen, Kate Simms, Sandra Dijkstra, Kevan Lyon, Nicholas Kristof, Ian Buruma, Jasper Becker, Maarten Valken, Andy Hsiao, Joel Ariaratnam, and of course Jeannette Ringold.

Finally, the book would never have become what it is without the many people who read it and looked at it so carefully. Many thanks to the trained eyes of photo editor Nicole Robbers and layout editor Stella Smienk, and the critical comments of Marije Wilmink, Stefan Landsberger, the late Frederik

Kossmann, Eveline Imelman, and Marieke van Oostrom. Thanks to Jaime Helegua for printing Vincent Mentzel's photos.

My deepest gratitude goes to Bettina Abraham, without whom this book would never have existed. She was the first to come up with the idea and has throughout the project provided me with frank and constructive criticism.

Beijing/The Hague, May 2006

Shenzhen